D0856503

RAND McNALLY

Chicago

A CELEBRATION

From high in the Sears Tower, this is the heart of the city at twilight. Lake Michigan and the evening sky make up the two blue hues just beyond the John Hancock Center (left of center).

Chicago

A CELEBRATION

Photography by Archie Lieberman
Text by Robert Cromie

RAND McNALLY
CHICAGO · NEW YORK · SAN FRANCISCO

The photographs in the book are dedicated to the memory of Kurt Murrow Lieberman and to the future of Noah Kurt Simpson Lieberman.

Chicago: A Celebration
General manager: Russell L. Voisin
Managing editor: Jon M. Leverenz
Editor: Elizabeth G. Fagan
Designer: Vito M. DePinto
Production editor: Laura C. Schmidt
Production manager: Patricia Martin

Chicago: A Celebration
Copyright © 1990 by Rand McNally & Company.
All rights reserved

Portions of this book originally appeared in *Chicago*, copyright © 1980 by Rand McNally & Company. No part of this publication may be reproduced, stored in a retrieval system, or transmitted, in any form or by any means—electronic, mechanical, photocopied, recorded, or other—without the prior written permission of Rand McNally. Printed in Italy.

Library of Congress Catalog Card Number: 90-53220
ISBN: 0-528-83414-2

From the Sears Tower observation floor, Chicago is bedecked in lights. Those familiar with the city will notice the University of Illinois at Chicago dimly lit below the left middle of the picture.

PREFACE

The first edition of Rand McNally's *Chicago* appeared just about ten years ago. The changing city has demanded new editions periodically; this revised version is the first since 1985. If left unwatched, the Windy City will take off and leave the static observer behind.

If you have been out of the Chicago area for even a very few years, and you eye the skyline upon your return, you will notice perhaps a dozen new highscrapers—the NBC Tower, 900 North Michigan, and the new Stone Container Building among them. Not to mention that the Merchandise Mart is in the process of a major overhaul; a new public library is being built; a new Comiskey Park is going up across the street from the old one; and the Adler Planetarium, Shedd Aquarium, Art Institute, and Chicago Historical Society are suddenly much bigger.

Furthermore, Mayor Harold Washington died suddenly around Thanksgiving, 1987, after serving only part of his second term. Alderman Eugene Sawyer succeeded him until an election brought Richard M. Daley to the position his father, Richard J. Daley, had occupied for so long.

It is, in fact, frustrating to try to keep track of this fast-moving city. Someone once said to an indefatigable and enthusiastic fellow who lugs his camera all over Chicago (and above it), at any hour, that there was no use trying to keep up with so many and so speedy a succession of changes.

There was a moment's pause, a brief look of dejection. Then a fleeting grin. "Just as long as they don't move the lake," he said.

ACKNOWLEDGMENTS

Without the help, guidance, permission, and kindness of the following people, many of the photographs in this book could not have been made: Chuck Adams, Jim Anderson, Maria Avery, Wilbur Barnes, Pete Barrett, Hank and Gilda Buchbinder, Chan Tha Sam, Dr. Urmilla Chaudry, Jerry Davis, Connie Day, Jim De Maria, Diane F. Dubey, Tom Duffy, Jim Egan, Jim Grice, Al Griminski, Sgt. Frank Gurgoni, Tim Hallan, David Hayman, John Hill, Bob Howell, Stan Humienny, Caroline Jansen, Mike Johnson, Charles A. Lindberg, Angelo Loukas, Karen Makowski, Pat Manthei, Lawrence L. Micelli, Helene Mores, Commander John Mulkerin, Steve Muniz, Rosie Navares, Sgt. Robert Notini, Sgt. James E. O'Boyle, Nancy M. Olszewski, Joe and Dorothy Palach, Keith Pamper, Joe Panico, Eddie Paquett, Sven Olaf Petersson, Ruth Rothstein, John Scalla, John Schlossman, Michael J. Siciliano, Alberta Simpson, Tony Skellin, Diann DeWeese Smith, John Stajic, Jack Star, David Stephenson, Sue Tornoi, Bernard Turnoi, Tina Vicini, Tom Weaver, Dave Woodcock

CONTENTS

Chicago: Yesterday and Today 8

Chicago: City by the Lake 26

Chicago: City at Work 64

Chicago: City of Arts and Sports 94

Chicago: People and Neighborhoods 134

A light show of moving neon tubes over the walkway greets travelers in the United Airlines terminal at O'Hare International Airport.

Chicago
YESTERDAY & TODAY

Archie Lieberman, the photographer whose inquisitive lenses have peered into the buildings, streets, and parks of Chicago at all hours and found many fine persons doing noteworthy things, explains the idea behind this volume.

"It is," he says firmly, "a *celebration* of Chicago."

Which explains why you won't find mournful mention of a number of things: the slums, the less-than-admirable high-rise housing projects, a police force that could use improvement, or a detailed account of the gun-noisy Prohibition days, when Al Capone and other mobsters grew rich and infamous. Attention won't be paid to the faults of the school system, and such unsavory topics as vote fraud (once a Chicago specialty), Operation Greylord which discovered judges on the take, scandal at various trading markets, and a number of shocking murders.

In short, there have been many unsavory events in the century and a half since the Windy City edged into existence as a tiny trading center. But this is the quieter tale of a lively and attractive town whose numerous credits and worthwhile happenings easily outweigh the demerits and the rogues we shall largely ignore.

By intriguing coincidence we just ran across a comment on a long-gone artist, Yoshio Markino, who some 80 years ago illustrated a book *The Colour of London.* M.H. Spielmann F.S.A., in his introduction, praises a winter scene depicting Chelsea on a snowy day and concludes:

"And if Mr. Markino has been kinder to our London slush than stern truth seems to demand, what need to complain? It is his painter's privilege to see with the eyes of the colourist and to ignore the mud." Mr. Lieberman and Mr. Markino would have liked each other.

Let the celebration continue!

It is improbable that there is such a creature as the average Chicagoan. For one thing, Chicagoans, because of the bracing Lake Michigan air, proper Midwestern food, and wise refusal to venture out on New Year's Eve, are far healthier than the rest of the population, and in particular, if you will pardon the chauvinism, New Yorkers. Healthy persons are far too busy to become like everyone else. Thus Chicago is a city of individuals.

Chicago has other advantages. For example, if you have to reach the airport in a hurry, O'Hare International Airport, said to be the world's busiest, is only about 25 minutes from downtown. Okay, longer during rush hour.

Another plus for Chicago. It is situated fairly close to the middle of the country, give or take 600 miles (if we've gone metric by the time you read this, make that 1,000 kilometers). So when you have to head out of town for some reason, you can do so in any direction without much danger of running into Newark.

A helicopter and some cooperation from the dying sun helped create this gold and purple portrait of the John Hancock Center and 900 North Michigan Avenue.

This photograph captures Wacker Drive and the Chicago River as it heads south just west of the Sears Tower.

Also, unless they figure out a way to dry up the lake, Chicago's water supply seems assured for centuries.

Even more important, Chicago's loyal sports fans would say, is that the city still has two major league baseball teams—the White Sox and the Cubs—although they don't always play as if they were; the legendary Chicago Bears; the Blackhawks; and the Bulls, recently rejuvenated by the sensational Michael Jordan. A colorful indoor soccer team—the Chicago Power—adds a dash of vitality to the scene, as do the consistently superior cage teams at DePaul and Loyola. The Power plays from November to March at the Rosemont Horizon.

The Chicago Cubs, while no longer playing all their games in daylight, have done extremely well at the gate since being acquired by the Chicago Tribune Company. Although they still are in quest of another pennant, which has eluded them for a number of years, they keep a firm grip on the world's most indefatigable group of fans, and the turnstiles keep clicking.

The White Sox, after an apparently genuine threat to move their franchise to the sunny South, where an appetizing prospect awaited, decided against the move when Gov. James Thompson and city officials offered an even more tempting package. Now the White Sox are leaving historic Comiskey Park—but only to move across the street to a new $100 million Comiskey Park which will seat 40,000 when home plate is dusted off for the first time in the spring of 1991. Nostalgia buffs will be happy that the new Comiskey Park will bear a family resemblance to the old.

Bill Veeck, the irrepressible maverick who twice owned the White Sox, no longer brightens the town, an irreparable loss. But he will always remain one of the most delightful Chicago originals.

A tip, before we go further: At the old Water Tower pumping station, Michigan and Chicago avenues, there is an office of the Chicago Convention and Tourism Bureau that offers sight-seeing advice and a variety of pamphlets, among them guides to shopping and dining in the city. It's worth a little trouble to stop by and pick them up and to take a look at the tower across the street, one of the few buildings in the path of the 1871 fire that survived.

What about the personality of Chicago itself? Chicago is a city of moods, most of them dictated by its will-o'-the-wisp weather. Sometimes it is happy and open; sometimes dour and forbidding. One day may be perfection, the sun's heat tempered by cool lake breezes. The next day the breezes have vanished, and the city swelters. Or there may be a storm of almost tropic intensity, with driving rain and fierce lightning.

Nor is beguiling Lake Michigan herself to be trusted. Beautiful but fickle, she may turn suddenly treacherous after a show of goodwill. Then small-boat warnings are hoisted and waves lash the beaches, occasionally roaring across Lake Shore Drive with a fury that makes travel hazardous or even impossible.

Also, there is the snow. During one unforgettable winter a few years ago, a Chicago record was set for the amount that came swirling down. Jane Byrne became

Chicago's first female chief executive, in large part because of the memory of day after day of impassable streets. She in turn lost in 1983 after a bitter campaign, to Congressman Harold Washington, the city's first black mayor.

One myth about the climate needs to be corrected, however. Chicago, in all fairness, is *not* the Windy City, despite its popular nickname. The latest edition of *The World Almanac* gives the average Chicago daily wind speed over a 12-month stretch as 10.3 mph with a top of 58 mph. Twelve United States weather stations recorded higher averages, and all 12 beat the 58-mile mark.

Note: It must be admitted that the first use of the Windy City appellation was made by an Easterner in reference to the propensity of Chicagoans to boast about their town. Nonetheless, in *most* cases it has been understood to mean that Chicago is a windy place. In any event, an ancient local maxim still holds: "If you don't like our weather, wait a minute!"

While the weather is unpredictable, often fooling even the finest forecasters, one facet of Chicago remains constant. It is, as most visitors will attest, a friendly town that goes out of its way to welcome and help strangers—a frontier trait, perhaps, that has lingered in this city long after having vanished from a great many other large communities in the country.

It is a city, too, where the people refuse to be overcome by disaster. Even while Chicago was burning in 1871, there was humor mixed with the fear and the occasional despair. The humor was wry but genuine, a preview of the same unquenchable spirit that Londoners were to display, like the unfurling of a battle flag, when the Nazi bombs came screaming down two-thirds of a century later.

The Great Chicago Fire (usually capitalized by true Chicagoans, who seem to regard it with a sort of snobbish approval) is the worst such catastrophe ever visited upon a United States city. The two-day holocaust, driven by demonic winds, leveled the business district and most of the town's finest residences. When the flames burned themselves out at Fullerton Avenue for lack of fuel, some 17,500 structures had been destroyed, 100,000 persons were homeless, and the total damage was estimated at $200 million, much of it covered by insurance that could not be paid. Wealthy men became paupers overnight, at least for a time, and an unknown number of persons died, perhaps as many as 300, although a total of only 120 bodies were recovered.

The full story of the Great Fire is one of heroism and cowardice, of generosity and avarice, of quick-witted actions, and of incredibly dim-witted ones. The man in charge of the water-purification crib, two miles out in the lake, battled flying embers for hours as his wife slept. But in the North Division, just above the river, Judge Joseph Easton Gary, ignoring the example of more prudent neighbors, refused to believe that the flames could reach his home—until the windowsills began to burn. By this time the roof of the pumping station (at the Water Tower) had collapsed, cutting off all hope that the fire department could end the blaze.

The noted evangelist, Dwight L. Moody, was among the first Northsiders to flee. His wife wanted to save the portrait of her husband painted by the well-known artist G.P.A. Healy. When Moody refused to remove it from the wall, Mrs. Moody had to ask a stranger to save the painting. "Take down my picture?" Moody scoffed. "Well, that would be a joke. Suppose I meet some friends in the same trouble as ourselves, and they say: 'Hullo, Moody, glad you have escaped; what's that you have saved and cling to so affectionately?' Wouldn't it sound well to reply, 'Oh, I've got my own portrait'?"

The stubborn optimism during and after the conflagration also is worth noting. Even before the fire had ended, someone was seen checking the ruins of the Reynolds Block to determine whether the jumbled bricks had cooled enough to be used again.

A chestnut-seller appeared Tuesday morning, while the embers still smoldered, at her old location on Lake Street, the first Chicagoan to reopen for business in the burned-over area.

And a merchant sent a telegram that same day to his wife, who was visiting in New York City:

Store and contents, dwelling and everything lost. Insurance worthless. See————immediately; tell him to buy all the coffee he can and ship this afternoon by express. Don't cry.

As another example of the sturdy Chicago character, consider Chaucey B. Blair, president of the Merchants' National Bank, who attended a meeting with fellow bankers immediately after the fire. Someone suggested the possibility of paying 25 cents for each dollar on deposit in pre-fire accounts. Blair ended the discussion in a hurry. "If a dollar is found in the vaults of the Merchants' National when they are reached and opened," he said crisply, "that dollar belongs to the depositors."

An editorial in the *Tribune* two days after the fire set the tone for most Chicagoans:

All is not lost. Though four hundred million dollars' worth of property has been destroyed, Chicago still exists. She was not a mere collection of stone, and bricks, and lumber....The great natural resources are all in existence; the lake, with its navies, the spacious harbor, the vast empire of...trade and commerce, all remain unimpaired, undiminished, and all ready for immediate resumption....*

We have lost money—but we have saved life, health, vigor and industry....

Let the watchword henceforth be: CHICAGO SHALL RISE AGAIN!

In November, Joseph Medill of the *Tribune* was elected mayor, perhaps because of that newspaper's optimistic editorial, but more probably because he ran on the "fireproof" (Union-Fireproof) ticket.

Back now to the beginnings.

A number of Indian trails converged or crossed in the swampy wilderness area that was to become Chicago. It was a natural place for travelers to meet, since Lake Michigan (then called Lake Illinois) was close at hand on

* *Later estimates put the figure at $200 million.*

The Magnificent Mile begins at the north end of the Michigan Avenue Bridge. The turret-topped building is 900 North Michigan Avenue. Most visitors to the Windy City find their way to the Magnificent Mile, with its tempting array of shops and hotels.

the east, and a portage of perhaps two-and-a-half miles to the west bridged the gap between the Chicago and Des Plaines rivers. The Des Plaines joined the Illinois, and that waterway led into the seemingly endless Mississippi.

While it is certain that some French *coureurs de bois* were familiar with the Chicago region even earlier, the first white men known to have stopped there were Louis Jolliet and Père Jacques Marquette. Jolliet, a young resident of Quebec, had been authorized by the French governor to explore the great river known to lie somewhere west of Lake Illinois. Father Marquette, a Jesuit missionary from Quebec who already had established missions for the Indians at Sault Ste. Marie and St. Ignace—later to become Michigan towns—was invited by Jolliet to accompany him.

The party left St. Ignace in the spring of 1673 and reached the Mississippi by way of the Fox and Wisconsin rivers. It was on the return journey that they passed through the Chicago area. Marquette came back, in 1674, on his way to pay a promised visit to the Kaskaskia Indians, and was trapped by winter. He and two companions built a cabin near the future site of Chicago, where they remained from early December until late March. Then the 38-year-old priest, now very ill, started back for St. Ignace; but on May 18, 1675, he died near Ludington, Michigan.

The next visitor of note was René Robert Cavelier, Sieur de La Salle, who had been given exclusive trading rights in the Mississippi Valley by the French. La Salle came through in 1681, using the Chicago portage on his way to the mouth of the Mississippi, where, in the magnificently offhand manner of explorers of the day, he claimed all of the lands fed by the Mississippi or its tributaries in the name of Louis XIV, King of France, naming the king's new land Louisiana. La Salle was later made its governor. After a futile attempt to found a French colony at the mouth of the Mississippi, La Salle was murdered by rebellious followers. He was 44 years old.

There is little to record about Chicago during the next century or so, other than that Jean Baptiste Point du Sable, whose mother was said to be a native of Haiti, became Chicago's first resident when he built a house on the river about 1784 and went into trade. His arrival was the beginning of a permanent settlement.

Other traders arrived, and during 1803 and 1804 Fort Dearborn was built and garrisoned. Du Sable had sold out by this time to Jean La Lime; and another very active trader, John Kinzie, came to town from St. Joseph, Michigan, in 1804. Despite the presence of a government trading post, which opened in 1805, private trade flourished. By 1806, with private trading firmly established, tobacco and butter each sold for 50 cents a pound, flour for 10 cents a pound, and whiskey for 50 cents a quart.

Kinzie's trade prospered but was halted abruptly by two circumstances: the War of 1812 and the fact that he killed his rival La Lime in a knife fight, probably in self-defense, and was forced to flee to Milwaukee.

During the late summer of 1812, Captain Nathan Heald, the Fort Dearborn commander, received word that an Indian attack on the fort was probable. When

Noontime jam at the elevated platform on Lake Street.

This panorama, which faces west and north, was shot from the Carbide and Carbon Building on Michigan Avenue. Easily spotted are the Sears Tower with sunlit antennae on the left, Marina City's twin cylinders in the center, and the John Hancock Center on the right.

various uprisings and the capture by Indians of Fort Mackinac underlined the warning, Heald was ordered to evacuate the post.

On August 15, 1812, a group of 55 regulars and a "militia" consisting of 12 men, accompanied by 9 women and 18 children, left Fort Dearborn for the distant safety of Fort Wayne. They were accompanied by an escort of about 30 Miami Indians. A mile and half on the way, several hundred hostile Indians were spotted among the sand dunes. As the fighting began, the Miami escort fled.

The little party had no chance. When the shooting stopped in what had been part battle and part massacre, 26 of the regulars were dead, as were the militiamen, two women, and 12 of the children. The rest surrendered. Captain Heald and his wounded wife survived. Fort Dearborn was set ablaze that night and was not rebuilt until 1816-17.

When the fort was again in use, a few traders drifted back. The fort continued its curiously haphazard existence for a few more years and was finally abandoned, an indication of the growing security of the village.

By 1825-26 there were 14 taxpayers in Chicago and 35 voters, with $8,000 in taxable property. There was no town government as such until 1833, however, when Chicago was incorporated as a village with a population of just over 400 people.

In 1833 with the defeat of Black Hawk, the Indians lost title to all their land between lower Lake Michigan and the Mississippi, and a brief land boom began. An English visitor to Chicago in 1834, three years before its incorporation as a city, saw the town as "one chaos of mud, rubbish and confusion." But, muddy as it was, the village grew, and Chicagoans seem to have been content. An elderly woman, in a nostalgic mood, once remarked: "The early settlers in Chicago were among the happiest people in the world!"

The town's first newspaper, the *Chicago Democrat*, began publishing in 1833, the same year that improvements in the channel permitted lake craft to enter the river. By 1835 the census estimated that there were 100 merchants in the city, 35 lawyers, and 25 physicians. The total population was 3,265.

The real-estate boom increased to frenzied proportions in 1836 when the first shovelful of earth was dug for the long-delayed Illinois and Michigan Canal, which was to link Chicago with the Mississippi River system. Even before this, Gurdon S. Hubbard, a Chicago business leader, was reported to have sold for $80,000 land that, less than five years earlier, had cost him $66.66. A depression slowed everything down in 1837, however, and again fortunes slipped away. Work on the canal was halted by a cholera epidemic in 1838 and by lack of money in 1842. But the canal finally was opened on April 16, 1848.

Other things added to Chicago's amazing growth and increasing reputation as a transportation, manufacturing, and business center. In 1847 Cyrus McCormick built his reaper factory with a borrowed $100,000 and soon had 120 people working for him. The following year the Galena and Chicago Union Railroad made its maiden run. A week later it puffed its way to the Des Plaines River, returning with a load of grain. Very soon the railroad was earning some $2,000 monthly. The year 1848 also brought electric telegraph service to Chicago.

The 1850 census had shown a population of 29,964. At the start of 1854, the population was more than 60,000, and the Galena and Chicago was carrying more grain than the Illinois and Michigan Canal. The Michigan Southern and Michigan Central railroads had reached Chicago in 1852, bringing New York to within a two-day journey. By 1855 there were 96 trains arriving daily, with 10 main rail lines and a number of branch lines in operation. On the other side of the scoresheet was a less impressive record. Cholera and smallpox still were common, and Chicago's death rate now led the nation.

It soon became obvious that rails were to be more important to Chicago's future than sails or steamships, even though in 1856 a cargo vessel loaded with wheat

from Liverpool anchored in the Chicago River. But already grain shipments by train in and out of the city amounted to 21 million bushels. Chicago was on the way to becoming the railroad capital of the nation.

Along with the rapid growth came problems to be solved. The city directory of 1857 listed 80 ballrooms and only 50 churches. Mayor "Long John" Wentworth personally led a raid on the Sands, a run-down area of disputed ownership north of the river, where vice, gambling, and poverty went hand in hand. The police tore down some buildings, others "caught" fire, and the residents scattered to various parts of the city.

Chicago, the city built on a swamp, already had raised a number of its streets out of the mire, probably giving an unknowing observer the impression that the buildings had begun sinking. The sidewalks varied so much in elevation that a visitor in 1855-56 wrote: "The profile of a Chicago sidewalk would resemble the profile of the Erie Canal where the locks are most plenty [*sic*]." Eventually it became necessary also to raise a number of buildings to bring them up to the street and sidewalk levels. Among these was the four-story Tremont House, a brick structure. The owners had been told the project would prove impossible. George M. Pullman, however, who had done similar work in the East, was equal to the task. He put 5,000 jackscrews and hundreds of workers into the basement and raised the Tremont almost seven feet, a fraction of an inch at a time, reportedly without even disturbing the guests.

By 1860 the population had reached 109,260. That was the year the old Sauganash Tavern at Lake and Market streets was demolished to make room for the Wigwam, the great wooden convention hall that was built in a record five weeks to attract the Republican convention. It was here that Abraham Lincoln, with help from the *Chicago Tribune,* was nominated for President.

Then came the Civil War. The death of Colonel Elmer E. Ellsworth—a dashing, colorful Chicagoan—brought the war home to Illinois. By July, 1861, with the conflict only three months old, Illinois had four times as many men prepared to join the Northern forces as could be handled readily. By the end of the war, Illinois had sent 231,488 into service—the best record among Northern states on a per capita basis. Of these, Chicago provided 20,000 out of its total population of about 110,000 when war broke out, and only a handful of that number were conscripts. Foreign-born Chicagoans enlisted readily, and a black infantry regiment, the 29th Illinois from Chicago, saw combat in Virginia.

Among those who served in the military were thousands of farm workers. The invention of the McCormick reaper had freed them for duty; the work on the farms would continue. Edwin M. Stanton, the Secretary of War, was quoted as saying, "Without McCormick's invention, I feel the North could not win and that the Union would be dismembered."

On May 1, 1865, Lincoln came to Chicago for the last time. A throng estimated at 125,000 filed past his bier as he lay in state in the Courthouse for a day and a night.

After the war, Chicago boasted 27 bridges across the river, a network of horse-car lines, a burgeoning population, and the world's greatest stockyards, which had opened in 1865. The Great Fire of 1871 slowed the city's growth only momentarily...

When the fire was over, help came from everywhere. New York, Cincinnati, Buffalo, St. Louis, and other cities responded. President Grant personally gave $1,000; the hackdrivers of Washington, D.C., and the crew of the *U.S.S. Vermont* each donated a day's pay; 23 foreign countries sent a total of $973,892.80. Thomas Hughes, the noted author of *Tom Brown's Schooldays,* gathered 8,000 books in England to help restock the city's public library. Among those contributing to the library were Dante Gabriel Rossetti, Disraeli, and Her Royal Highness, Queen Victoria.

The city's recovery was phenomenal. Within a week after the fire there were 5,497 temporary buildings in use and 200 permanent ones under construction. During the next year 10,000 new buildings were in various stages of readiness. By 1873 grain shipments were 50 percent above the pre-fire level and the Union Stockyards, which had escaped the flames completely, butchered twice as many hogs in 1872 as in 1870. By the late 1870s such firms as Armour and Company; Libby, McNeill and Libby; and Morris and Co. were shipping vast quantities of meat to the eastern seaboard in the new refrigerated cars.

Chicago was growing with incredible speed. The 1880 census showed a population of 503,185, an increase of more than 200,000 in 10 years. As usual in the nation's most unpredictable city, the unusual continued to happen.

The most memorable event of the decade was the tragic Haymarket Riot of 1886. Chicago had become the center of the labor movement. A general strike had been called on May 1. On May 3, six strikers at the McCormick Reaper Works had been killed as a result of police intervention. A protest meeting was called by a prolabor group, described by some as anarchists, at Haymarket Square on the near West Side for the evening of May 4. About 3,000 persons, including Mayor Carter Henry Harrison, Sr., showed up. The crowd started to thin, however, as rain began to fall. Harrison observed for a while, then stopped at the nearby Des Plaines Street police station to suggest that the gathering seemed to be a peaceable one and that the waiting police reserves probably would not be needed. But shortly thereafter, for reasons never fully explained, an inspector ordered 175 police officers to the scene, and the crowd was commanded to disperse. A bomb was thrown—no one ever found out by whom—and the explosion and ensuing gunfire left seven policemen fatally wounded and scores of other persons hurt.

Hundreds of persons were questioned and many jailed for a time. Eventually, nine men were indicted for murder, although one already had fled to Europe, and charges against another were dropped when he turned over evidence to the State. Chicago and the world followed the trial throughout the summer, and while nothing was presented which linked the defendants directly to whomever threw the bomb, an angry and possibly "packed" jury returned guilty verdicts against all seven. Judge Joseph E. Gary sentenced one defendant to 15 years imprisonment and ordered the others hanged.

One man killed himself in his cell, and the day before the execution Gov. Richard Oglesby commuted two of the sentences to life terms. The remaining three were hanged, despite a storm of well-reasoned protests from across the world and the feeling by many Chicagoans that the trial had been a mockery.

Six years after the trial, Gov. John Peter Altgeld, a man of unswerving integrity, pardoned the remaining three, even though this action effectively ended his own political career.

The year 1886 also marked the beginning of a sort of comic-opera sketch when George Wellington Streeter ran his excursion boat into a sandbar near Chicago Avenue. Finding he couldn't free it, Streeter decided to live on board with his wife. He also decided, as the sand began filling in around the boat, that the land thus created was his. Efforts to force him out failed for years, despite court action and police raids, and he even sold lots in Streeterville (as the district became known) before he finally left under duress in 1918. The Furniture Mart and Northwestern University's downtown campus now stand on land that Cap Streeter once "owned."

By 1890, with the city increasing its area from about 35 to 178 square miles, the official population passed the million mark, a jump of more than 100 percent in 10 years. Chicago was now the second largest city in the country and wildly enthusiastic about a new and alluring prospect: playing host to the projected World's Columbian Exposition.

The giant fair, authorized by Congress to commemorate the 400th anniversary of the discovery of the New World by Columbus, was opened to the public on May 1, 1893. Scores of foreign countries and all of the states and territories were represented.

The exposition covered 533 acres of Jackson Park and the Midway Plaisance (now the heart of the University of Chicago campus), with the amusement concessions and some of the minor buildings built on another 80 acres between Jackson and Washington parks. The attractions there ranged from the giant Ferris wheel, invented by Pittsburgh railroad and bridge engineer G.W.G. Ferris, to Little Egypt, the belly dancer.

It is impossible to do more than hint at the wonders of the great fair, about which books have been written. There was the giant Krupp gun, which weighed 127 tons and had a range of 16 miles (but accuracy only up to 14); there were 60 Venetian gondoliers; there were Indians and Esquimaux, 280,000 tulips, and a Japanese Village on the Wooded Island, which also had a replica of Davy Crockett's cabin. The fair boasted paintings by Corot, Millet, Constable, Rousseau, Copley, Stuart, and many other of the world's leading artists. There was a Manufacturers Building, where four times the available space had been sought by 59 countries. There was the Woman's Building, designed by a 22-year-old woman from Boston, architect Sophia G. Hayden. Panama hats were woven on the spot by Colombian natives. Mexico brought a 45-piece band; Palestine had Syrian horsemen and native dancers; and Alaska displayed an impressive sea-otter pelt valued at $500. Throughout the length and breadth of the great fair, marvels abounded.

Trains and boats carried visitors to the grounds, which stretched for about two miles along the lakefront. There were movable sidewalks, an indoor ice-skating rink, and captive balloons that rose to 1,000 feet at the cost of $1 per ride. The various restaurants could feed 60,000 persons every hour. The American Bible Society gave away 250,000 copies of the New Testament. Probably the Ferris wheel was the greatest noncultural attraction. It was 250 feet in diameter and had 36 passenger cars, each capable of holding 60 persons. From the top of the wheel, riders on a clear day could view portions of Illinois, Wisconsin, Indiana, and Michigan.

The exposition lasted until October 30, 1893. Attendance built up rapidly as enthusiastic visitors spread the word. The final total was 27,529,400 visitors, of whom more than 700,000 crowded the grounds on Chicago Day. A remark by an elderly visitor to his wife seemed to sum up the general feeling of those who came to the fair. "Well, Susan," he said, "it paid, even if it did take all the burial money."

The fair ended on a tragic note, however. On October 28 Mayor Carter Henry Harrison, Sr., was shot and killed by a deranged job seeker.

At the beginning of the 20th century, Chicago had an area of about 190 square miles, and the census for 1900 showed a population of 1,698,575, of which 587,112 were foreign born. Germans led the list with 170,738, followed by Irish, 73,912; Polish, 59,713; Swedish, 48,836; Bohemian (including Moravian, Ruthenian, and Slovak), 36,362; Canadian, 34,799; English, 29,308; Russian, 24,178; and Norwegian, 22,011. Thirty-seven other countries or regions (such as Asia and South and Central America) contributed to Chicago's growth as well. The number of blacks increased to 30,150 from 14,271 in 1890, but the number of American Indians had dwindled from 14 to 8. There also was a group of 315 Chicagoans who fell into a wildly romantic category: Born at Sea.

Chicago was a bustling, booming city as it entered the 20th century. It was growing culturally, as well as commercially. The first "little theater" in the nation was erected for the Hull House Players. The city had 12 daily newspapers. Orchestra Hall was opened. For a dozen years, until it was superseded by Hollywood, Chicago was the leading production center for the fledgling motion picture industry. Essanay Studios shot pictures here with Wallace Beery, Gloria Swanson, Francis X. Bushman, Ben Turpin, and others.

But many of the events of the early 20th century were somber ones. Five days after Christmas in 1903 Eddie Foy was starring in *Mr. Bluebeard* at the Iroquois Theater when fire broke out on stage. The audience rushed in panic for the exits. By the time help arrived, 571 persons, most of them women and children, were dead in the nation's worst theater blaze.

An afternoon scene along the Magnificent Mile. The Old Water Tower, spotlighted by the sun, is a survivor of the Great Fire of 1871. Another century-old relic is the pumping station across Michigan Avenue.

Between 1895 and 1914 Carter Henry Harrison, Jr., served five terms as Mayor of Chicago. Then, in 1915, the voters were somehow bamboozled into naming William Hale (Big Bill) Thompson for the city's top office. Big Bill was bombastic, egocentric, and during World War I, very pro-German and anti-Allies. But there was an even worse civic disaster that year. On July 24 the steamer *Eastland,* while being loaded at its Chicago River pier with a merry crowd of employees about to sail on the annual Western Electric picnic, suddenly capsized, drowning 812 of the nearly 2,000 aboard. Among those planning to join the throng before the *Eastland* sailed was young George Halas, later to become the owner of the Chicago Bears. He was delayed and failed to board.

In 1919 there was a vicious race riot, triggered by the death of a young black youth who ventured into what white roughnecks considered a "restricted" area along the lakeshore. The white boys kept forcing him back into the water as he tried to reach a raft. The young black drowned. Before the rioting ended five days later, with the arrival of state militia that Mayor Thompson was pressured into sending for, 23 blacks and 14 whites had died.

Later in the year the White Sox lost a strangely listless World Series to the Cincinnati Reds, and rumors sprang up almost immediately that the games had been "fixed." Many months afterward, eight of the White Sox players were indicted, among them "Shoeless" Joe Jackson, the great outfielder, whose name has become immortal not only because of his hitting ability, but also because of the dejected little boy who spotted Joe on the Courthouse steps after he had been accused and supposedly cried, "Say it isn't so, Joe!" All eight so-called "Black Sox," although found not guilty, were barred from organized baseball for life.

Two months after the armistice ended World War I, the Prohibition amendment was ratified. The country went dry (officially, that is) a year later, early in 1920, contributing greatly to the growth of Chicago's gangs. Chicago's reputation became linked with gangs and violence. Al Capone emerged as the leading figure among Chicago's criminal elite. He was courted by some of the community's leading citizens, given preferential treatment by the police, and even photographed at Wrigley Field chatting amiably with one of the town's finest ballplayers.

Big Bill Thompson, with hoodlum support, defeated the reform mayor, William E. Dever, in 1927 to regain his City Hall office. Thompson had campaigned on an anti-British platform, threatening to punch King George V in the nose, if opportunity offered. He decried the existence of "pro-British" books in the schools, books that had been purchased during his administration. He even supported an abortive attempt to burn some of the "pro-British" books that were in the public library. But no one could be found to light the match.

Chicago's reputation grew even worse for a while. In the 1929 St. Valentine's Day Massacre, seven members of the George (Bugs) Moran gang (Moran and Capone were rivals) were lined up and gunned down in a North Clark Street garage. And in 1930, on a lovely June day, Alfred (Jake) Lingle, a *Chicago Tribune* crime reporter, was shot and killed in the Randolph Street underpass to the Illinois Central station. His murder was at first taken to be a warning to Chicago newsmen to deter them from attacks on gang forces. It later turned out to be the elimination of a newspaperman with strong underworld ties and a great deal of unexplained wealth.

Time was running out on Capone, who no longer was considered acceptable by most Chicagoans. In 1931 he was sentenced to 11 years in the penitentiary for income-tax evasion. He died in Florida in 1947, ravaged by syphilis, his mind gone.

Anton J. (Tony) Cermak, supported by all but the Hearst papers, defeated Big Bill Thompson in 1931. Cermak, who presided at the Chicago convention that nominated Franklin Roosevelt in 1932, later was invited to Florida by the president-elect. On February 15, 1933, Cermak was fatally wounded by a crazed gunman, Giuseppe Zangara, whose target was Roosevelt. After he was hit, Cermak supposedly murmured to FDR, "I'm glad it was me instead of you."

Forty years after the World's Columbian Exposition, the city staged another mammoth fair. The Century of Progress Exposition, celebrating the 100th anniversary of Chicago's formal existence, was held on the lakefront south of Grant Park between 12th and 23rd streets. The spectacle, while not to be compared with its predecessor in excellence, had numerous inspiring attractions. There was fan dancer Sally Rand, the fair's answer to the Columbian Exposition's Little Egypt. Another popular attraction was the Midget Village, whose residents included 83-year-old Jennie Quigley, who also had appeared at the 1893 exposition. Other, more cerebral, exhibits also were plentiful. Although the fair got off to a slow start, eventually, in two seasons, paying customers totaled more than 39 million.

Among those visiting the Century of Progress, or so he told his friends, was John Dillinger, Public Enemy No. 1. He also said he had posed for his photograph with an unsuspecting police officer on the exposition grounds. Dillinger, the former Indiana farm boy, was shot and killed by G-men as he left the Biograph Theater on Lincoln Avenue July 22, 1934. There was a woman on his arm as he walked to his death—the same one who had betrayed him to the Feds—"The Lady in Red."

Chicago moved into the 1940s. Although it was known only to a few scientists and highly placed govern-

In 1986 the Stone Container Corporation moved into this building with the diamond-shaped roof. Nine floors of the 43-story edifice on Michigan Avenue are occupied by Stone Container personnel.

One of the newest structures in the city is the subway terminal at O'Hare International Airport. Note the Chicago Police Department's canine mass-transit unit on the right.

The Widow Clarke's house was built on Michigan Avenue near 16th Street in 1836 by Henry B. Clarke, banker and hardware entrepreneur. It is the city's oldest building. About 1871, shortly before the Great Fire, the house was moved to 4526 South Wabash. Since then it has been moved twice and restored. Clarke House is now part of the Prairie Avenue Historic District near 18th and Calumet.

ment officials, the first nuclear chain reaction, which led to the making of the atomic bomb, occurred in a small laboratory at the University of Chicago on December 2, 1942. The bomb didn't become public knowledge until it had wiped out Hiroshima in August, 1945, precipitating the surrender of Japan and the end of World War II.

After the war, Chicago continued to boom. By 1949 Meigs Field, a small lakefront airport, was opened on Northerly Island near the Adler Planetarium, giving small aircraft a landing spot with easy access to the Loop. In 1955 Richard J. Daley, 52 years old, beat a World War II combat veteran, Robert E. Merriam, a University of Chicago professor and Hyde Park alderman, to begin Daley's occupancy of the mayor's office, which lasted until his

OPPOSITE
Busy day on the Chicago River. A U.S. Coast Guard helicopter and small craft stage a mock rescue operation, while crews practice as preparations are underway for the Oxford-Cambridge annual race, held for the first time in Chicago in 1989. The Chicago Sun-Times *Building and one of the twin towers of Marina City are in the background.*

CHICAGO SUN-TIMES
COLUMBUS DRIVE
41467
CALUMET HARBOR

death in 1976. His regime coincided with a period of expansion and good business and a popular view of Chicago as "The City That Works."

Fortune magazine, in a 1955 article, had this to say about the city:

Right now the most exciting city in the U.S. is Chicago, Illinois. What is happening in Chicago amounts, in many ways, to a rebuilding of the city....All over the city there is a fury of blasting and leveling. And, as the girders go up for the new overpasses, office buildings, factories, apartments, stores, and hospitals, even the most skeptical Chicagoan, hardened against mere rhetoric...must now conclude that the city means business.

An example of the new business spirit was a huge convention center, McCormick Place, which opened in 1960. The $35 million building burned to the ground in 1967 but was succeeded by a far larger $75 million structure in 1971, needed to maintain Chicago's reputation as a trade and convention capital.

The city continued to be the transporation hub of the nation, the world's largest railroad center, the banking and insurance center of the Midwest, and its largest medical center. Following the completion of the St. Lawrence Seaway in 1959 and construction of huge dock and storage facilities on Lake Calumet, Chicago was one of the world's largest inland seaports. About 200 ships arrive yearly from 42 foreign countries. Helen A. Brohl, Director of Marketing and Maritime, for the Illinois International Port, says Chicago ranks 22d among the nation's ports. Midway Airport, in southwest Chicago, was succeeded as the city's principal airport in the 1960s by O'Hare International Airport, still the busiest in the world.

Chicago's skyline underwent fantastic changes, reflecting the influence and leadership of a new school of architecture led by Ludwig Mies van der Rohe and other architects who fled with him to Chicago from Germany. Among the new buildings were the entire campus of the University of Illinois at Chicago (formerly Circle Campus or UICC); new structures at the Illinois Institute of Technology, the University of Chicago, and Northwestern University; and the Prudential Building. The architectural renaissance continued in the 1970s, frequently with far taller structures, including the 80-story marble-covered Amoco Oil Building, the 60-story First National Bank Building, the 100-story John Hancock Center, and the 110-story Sears Tower, the tallest structure in the world upon its completion in 1974. North Michigan Avenue, Chicago's "Magnificent Mile," kept developing as an important shopping area, especially after the opening in 1977 of the elegant shopping complex known as Water Tower Place, which incidentally houses a Ritz-Carlton Hotel. On the site of Jean Baptiste Point du Sable's rude cabin stands the 40-story Equitable Building and a broad plaza known as Pioneer Court, an ideal place to view the skyline and the river and to contemplate the changes that have occurred in Chicago since 1784.

Horse-drawn carriages wait for customers near Water Tower Place. Loyola University's Water Tower campus provides the backdrop.

OPPOSITE
These are some of the many bridges over the Chicago River. The 160-year-old Oxford-Cambridge race, usually run on the Thames, covered two miles on the Chicago River in 1989. It started from Riverside Plaza and ended at Cityfront Center, east of Columbus Drive. A staggered start was necessary because of a narrow bend on the course.

Panoramic vista looking south from an apartment window at 2800 Lake Shore Drive.
Note the apartment buildings on the near right, and in the distance, the ever-changing downtown skyline.

Chicago
CITY BY THE LAKE

This is a view from the Hancock. Here the Outer Drive sweeps past the famous Drake Hotel (lower right, beyond the Playboy Building). Oak Street Beach parallels the Drive, and the high-rise apartments offer beautiful and expensive views of Lake Michigan.

The presence of Lake Michigan along 25 miles of Chicago's sunrise border is perhaps the single feature of their city of which Chicagoans are most proud. Nowhere else in the world is there a comparable urban stretch of such unsullied magnificence, put to such a perfect use.

Lake Michigan is, of course, one of the reasons for Chicago's great importance as a commercial and manufacturing center. Sailing ships or freighters have carried cargo of all kinds to and from the city for more than a century. But this is not why the lake and its shoreline are so appealing to most Chicagoans. There are other, more personal, attractions.

If you are in quest of museums, theaters, an incredible variety of sea creatures under one roof, or a building large enough to hold a trade show or convention; if you want to loaf in the park, shoot at targets, look at a long pier or peer at a short airport, swim, fish, go boating, listen to rock or symphony music, or be soothed by the splash and sparkle of a great fountain; if you'd like to play golf, tennis, baseball, bocce, handball, chess, pitch horseshoes, wander through the zoo, watch a football game, introduce your youngsters to a farmyard filled with friendly animals, or view the splendid Lincoln Park Conservatory; or if you simply have an unaccountable desire to board a German submarine, go down into a coal mine, or do a bit of stargazing, even though it's high noon—all these and other entertainments await you beside, in, on, or near the lake.

There are some Chicagoans, too, for whom the lakefront is where one goes to get into a good mood or minister to a bad one. Others ignore everything along the shoreline except the Outer Drive, which still is a scenic way to get into or out of town, except on stormy occasions when the lake washes across sections of the highway.

Part of the credit for preserving this golden strip along the water belongs to Daniel H. Burnham, the architect who created the Burnham Plan for the city, a plan that was sponsored and backed by the most influential members of the business community. A portion of the credit goes also to Aaron Montgomery Ward, the mail-order millionaire, who was almost fanatical in his successful efforts to keep construction away from the eastern edge of Lake Park (renamed Grant Park in 1901).

Burnham's plan was adopted by the City Council in 1909. Among his suggestions were the setting aside of some 20 miles of lakeshore for parks and other public use, the widening of various boulevards, putting highways below some portions of Michigan Avenue and Wacker Drive, the building of Navy Pier and the Union railroad station, and the creation of Cook County's enviable forest preserve system. Obviously, Burnham lived up to his own advice: "Make no little plans. They have no magic to stir men's blood."

Much of the lakefront, as it now is, came about through a natural buildup of sand, as in the case of Streeterville. But even more of it is "made" land. Immediately after the Great Chicago Fire, vast quantities of rubble and other debris were dumped into the water at Lake (Grant) Park, building up the eroding shoreline. In the years immediately following Burnham's proposals, the city bought privately held shore property and acquired about four miles of very choice lakefront land east of the business district, which was owned by the Illinois Central Railroad. The filling in of the shoreline continued for decades, with materials from building excavations, river dredging, and the city dump. The eventual placement along the lake, east and a little south of the Loop, of the Field Museum of Natural History, Soldier Field, the Shedd Aquarium, and the Adler Planetarium was made possible by this early protection of the shoreline.

The lakefront is a long stretch of beaches and parks. One of the most beautiful of the city's 563 parks, Lincoln, is located a few miles north of the business district. The land, which was bought from the state in 1834, was first utilized as a cemetery. It was turned into a park in 1868. Restrictions were established to make the park a safe recreation area. For example, it was illegal to travel through the area faster than six miles an hour. Then, in 1873, the speed limit on Lake Shore Drive through the park was lifted on Tuesday and Friday afternoons for the benefit of owners of fast horses.

The Lincoln Park Zoo began with a pair of swans donated by New York's Central Park in 1868; a bear cub was the first purchase. The zoo, which now attracts about 4 million visitors annually (a national record), has more than 2,000 animals, including a number of gorillas, and two koalas, on loan from the San Diego Zoo. Lincoln Park Zoo's 35 acres include a Kid's Corner, where youngsters and animals meet, and various workshops. The zoo is open daily.

The Lincoln Park Conservatory, on three-and-a-half acres adjoining the zoo, is famous for displays of azaleas in February and March, spring plants in April, mums in November, and Yuletide blossoms in December and January. Its counterpart on the West Side, the Garfield Park Conservatory, with four-and-a-half acres, has comparable shows four times yearly, and draws crowds from all parts of Chicagoland for its smashing Easter spectacular. Garfield has been called the world's most beautiful conservatory.

City parks provide an incredible variety of fun and instruction for the thousands of Chicagoans who use their facilities each year. In the larger parks are 253 fieldhouses, 182 gymnasiums, and 87 assembly halls. In addition to athletic fields and indoor and outdoor sports, there are provisions for learning a wide variety of skills,

The skyline seems crowded when inspected from this vantage point—west from Adler Planetarium across Monroe Harbor. With its split-diamond roof, the new Stone Container Building; on the right, the Prudential Insurance structure.

from macrame to cabinet work. Instruction is offered in such areas as piano, guitar, string-instrument repair, quilting, ceramics, woodworking, photography, and jewelry making.

Chicago boasts a wide range of museums. Among the major ones, the most consistently popular with visitors of all ages, from every state in the Union and 100 foreign countries, is the Museum of Science and Industry, which opened in 1933. It is located at 57th Street and Lake Shore Drive, occupying what was the Palace of Fine Arts building at the World's Columbian Exposition.

The Museum of Science and Industry entertains and instructs about 4 million visitors a year, many of them wide-eyed, fascinated children. The museum was made possible by Chicago's Julius Rosenwald, an early Sears, Roebuck and Co. partner, who initially donated $3 million for the creation of an industrial museum and whose later gifts totaled another $5 million.

The Museum of Science and Industry is one of the most entrancing places in the city, with fascinations at every turn for persons of any age. It is a do-it-yourself museum. There are cranks and buttons and levers all over the place, waiting to be turned or pushed or pulled. Each visitor can play tic-tac-toe with a computer (which usually wins), find out how gravity works without getting hit on the head by an apple, and become involved with many other oddments and marvels.

Here you can tour the U-505, a German submarine captured off the African coast by Captain Dan Gallery during World War II; go down into a coal mine; walk through a model of the human heart, 16 feet high; marvel at Colleen Moore's world-renowned dollhouse, now renamed the Fairy Castle; watch baby chicks emerge from their shells; see a circus both through film and the antics of 22,000 tiny figurines; or take a simulated flight in a space shuttle. And that's only a sample of the more than 2,000 exhibits that cover 400,000 square feet of space. There is no admission charge, even though the *New York Times* once lauded the Museum of Science and Industry as "the liveliest show in town."

There are, however, several *exhibits* to which admission is charged, the most spectacular of which is the Omnimax Theater, with changing film programs, in which viewers are subjected to such unique visual and sound effects that they feel themselves in the middle of whatever appears on the large-size screen. This is a new addition to the museum's series of amazements.

A word of warning: While the coal mine should not be missed, it's not for claustrophobes. The slow hoist that carries you down gives the impression of descending much deeper than the reality. Once down, you will see walls made of giant slabs of coal from southern Illinois and be given a demonstration of how miners work. A memorable experience for young or old—even if you hate to feel hemmed in.

Not far from the Museum of Science and Industry is the Oriental Institute of the University of Chicago, 1155 East 58th Street. It was founded in 1919 by James Henry Breasted, the noted Egyptologist. Since that time the Institute has sponsored well over 50 archeological expeditions to the Near East. Despite its name, the Institute does not concern itself with Japan, China, or India. Egypt, Syria, Turkey, Israel, Iraq, Iran, and their neighbors are as oriental as the Institute gets; if you stretch the point only slightly, you might call it the largest of all of Chicago's ethnic museums. The Institute has one of the finest collections in the world of ancient artifacts from the Near East. Its staff scholars are currently working on the multivolume Chicago Assyrian dictionary, of which 15 volumes have been issued, as well as dictionaries of Hittite and demotic languages. In 1980 the Institute sponsored a tour of Syria under the direction of John Carswell, then the Institute curator, who formerly taught at the University of Beirut. Karen L. Wilson, who has a Ph.D. in art and archeology of the Near East, has been curator since 1988. The museum is free and is closed on Mondays.

Another hidden gem is the Chicago Academy of Sciences at 2001 North Clark Street in Lincoln Park. It seems safe to say that most Chicagoans have never been inside; it definitely is safe to say that anyone who doesn't visit the Academy is missing a great deal. Life-sized dioramas and other exhibits relating to the natural history of the Great Lakes region include two walk-in areas, one depicting Chicago as a coal forest in 300,000,000 B.C. and the other, a simulated canyon.

The Field Museum of Natural History was started in the Palace of Fine Arts on the World's Columbian Exposition grounds and was moved into its present building just above Soldier Field in 1921. It is one of the world's best. There are more than 19 million specimens and artifacts, but, despite almost nine acres of exhibit space in the five-story building, only a small fraction (less than one-half of one percent) of the museum's treasures can be displayed at the same time.

It is impossible to describe adequately the contents of this giant storehouse. But they include many Indian relics, tools used 10,000 years ago in China, a full-scale Pawnee earth lodge, pottery from Pompeii, the skeleton of an albertosaurus, two huge elephants in combat, and new permanent exhibits such as Inside Ancient Egypt,

which has an exact replica of a multilevel tomb (complete with a grave-robber's tunnel), 23 mummies, and a 3,847-year-old boat which was owned by King Sen-wosret III. Another permanent exhibit, four years in the making, is Traveling the Pacific, which shows a coral isle, an outrigger canoe, a New Guinea village, and a modern Tahitian marketplace.

Within very easy walking distance of the Field Museum are two other buildings that are consistent attractions, both for Chicagoans and for visitors from across the world. A visit to the John G. Shedd Aquarium, for many persons, may be as rewarding as a visit to their favorite shrink. There is something peace-inducing and relaxing about watching fish swim slowly past—although there are a few that dart—or even playing the "Of-whom-does-that-fish-remind-you?" game. Chicago writer Sheldon Mix, in an article on the aquarium in *Chicago* magazine, maintained that he had discovered fish look-alikes for a number of celebrities.

There also is considerable allure, especially for the young, in the cannibal fish. Mix overheard a young lady delightedly inform her mother that the piranha at which they were gazing "can eat a big cow, or even *Daddy!*" Whatever the reason, the aquarium is a marvelous place to spend a few hours.

The most popular single attraction presently home to countless numbers of rarely motionless inhabitants (the moray eels and a few turtles sometimes tend to hang about a bit), is the Coral Reef, which cost $1.2 million to build and was opened in 1971. The tank measures 40 feet across and holds 90,000 gallons of sea water. A scuba diver from the museum staff feeds the Reef population twice daily (three times a day on weekends) and is very occasionally nipped by some creature whose appetite makes it careless.

The aquarium has freshwater fish, both cold and tropical, and enough other exhibits in the six galleries to total about 6,000 fish, representing more than 600 species. There are a fish-oriented library, classes for visiting schoolchildren, and various educational programs, in-

The annual Lakefront Air and Water Show drew this audience to North Avenue Beach for a reasonably uncrowded view of the spectacle.

The Chicago Police Department's marine unit lends a routine helping hand to a sailboat in need of a tow.

A father-and-daughter tableau highlights this summertime beach scene.

cluding summertime ones for both children and adults.

A $43 million, four-level Oceanarium, almost doubling the size of the aquarium, is scheduled to open in the fall of 1990. Shedd, which then will have 400,000 square feet of space, will become the world's largest aquarium. The new wing will contain a realistic replication of the western Pacific and southeastern Alaskan coastline, with trails through the rocky landscape and seating accommodations for 1,200 spectators. There will be five cold saltwater pools, the largest about 180 feet long, 80 feet wide, and 30 feet deep; this will hold four Pacific white-sided dolphins and three false killer whales. The other four pools will accommodate beluga whales, two of which already have been captured and are in Churchill, Manitoba, awaiting completion of their new home. Other sea creatures exhibited will include otters (two of them otter pups rescued from the 1989 Exxon oil spill), penguins, starfish, sea anemones, crabs, and mussels. There will be underwater viewing galleries, and amenities will include a restaurant, gift shop, library, and member's lounge.

A few hundred yards east of the aquarium is the Adler Planetarium, opened in 1930, which was made possible through the generosity of Max Adler, an official of Sears, Roebuck and Co., who decided to give Chicago a planetarium to rival the one that he and his wife had seen in Germany. Adler also donated a number of antique instruments used in astronomy, navigation, engineering, and timekeeping. These became the basis for the present museum collection, which is considered one of the finest in the world.

At the planetarium you can view the night sky as it is today or see it reproduced in the sky theater as it was over Bethlehem when Christ was born. You can also enroll in one of the many courses in astronomy and navigation offered by the planetarium; among them are ancient astronomy, navigation in local waters, sky photography, using the telescope, celestial navigation, making a telescope mirror, space colonies and space travel, meteorites and the solar system, searching for extraterrestrial life, and a teacher's workshop.

While at the Adler Planetarium you probably will wish to visit the dining area, which offers a re-creation of the moon's surface, with Earth and the Milky Way in the distance as they would appear if you were indeed peering out across the lunar landscape.

It is difficult to say enough about the pleasures afforded by the lakefront and Lake Michigan. Some of these have been described briefly. Others have been hinted at. And still there are more: water sports and boating, for example, whether of the short cruise or let's-go-to-Mackinaw variety; fishing for smelt or coho, a pastime that lures thousands of Chicagoans each year; the Chicago Marathon, an annual event, which is run in part through Grant Park; or simply sitting and watching the varying patterns fashioned by the Buckingham Fountain.

There are special events, such as the unprecedented appearance in Grant Park of Pope John Paul II, obviously a once-in-a-lifetime occurrence. Although figures vary, depending on the source, the Chicago Park District estimated that half a million of the faithful and the curious saw the pontiff on that occasion.

Then there are very popular, if less unusual, attractions such as the annual lakeshore Air and Water Show, staged in late July or August, or the series of concerts by the Grant Park Symphony Orchestra and Chorus, which begin late in June and continue for about two months, with several concerts weekly.

In addition there are privately sponsored rock concerts and other shows, the constantly changing sequence of athletic and other spectacles in Soldier Field, and the Taste of Chicago, created by scores of participating restaurants in Grant Park in July.

Along Chicago's lakefront, in every season of the year, there is something for every taste.

This cafe has only a few customers now, its menu is limited, and it folds if it rains. But someday it may outgrow Oak Street Beach, and the bicycles and skateboards will have to remain outside.

The Sears Tower is always overlooking something. In this instance, the imminent start of the 82nd annual Chicago-Mackinaw race, in which 281 craft participated. The distance covered was 333 miles, and it was the slowest contest in nearly 30 years because the wind refused to cooperate.

Café
B&B
The Drake

Lincoln Park lagoon is one of the favorite haunts of Chicagoans seeking a place to relax and forget. The building on the left (in the photo at right) is the Amoco Tower arrogantly shoving its way out of the scene. It is the second tallest building in the city.

Four views of Chicago's skyline from Diversey Harbor. Chicago anglers, though a hardy lot in spring and summer, head for home when the snow and ice arrive.

The city skyline and the sinking sun offer a magical setting for one of Grant Park's most consistent attractions: the ever-entrancing Buckingham Fountain, which was dedicated in 1946 and flows from May until October. Multicolored lights create an ever-changing spectacle.

Below: A gorilla in the Great Ape House, Lincoln Park Zoo.

Above and below: The Lincoln Park Conservatory, from the outside and the inside.

Soldier Field at sunset. The Chicago Bears have drawn sellout crowds here for many years, but there is talk of a new stadium for the Monsters of the Midway.

Nearby, John G. Shedd Aquarium is one of the lakefront's prime attractions. Soon it will be home to whales, dolphins, seals, and other saltwater creatures. The aquarium, largest indoor facility of its kind in the world, is closed only on Christmas and New Year's Day.

One of the ghosts from the World's Columbian Exposition of 1893, this is now the Museum of Science and Industry. It was also the first home of the Field Museum of Natural History and the exposition's Palace of Fine Arts.

Two enraged elephants dominate the main hall of the Field Museum. Many Chicagoans and visitors spend days exploring this museum.

For boat owners this is better than sighting the first robin. Spring is here for the nautical crowd when mooring buoys are set in Grant Harbor adjacent to Adler Planetarium.

Sculling on the Lincoln Park lagoon is only one of many ways to enjoy this beautiful park.

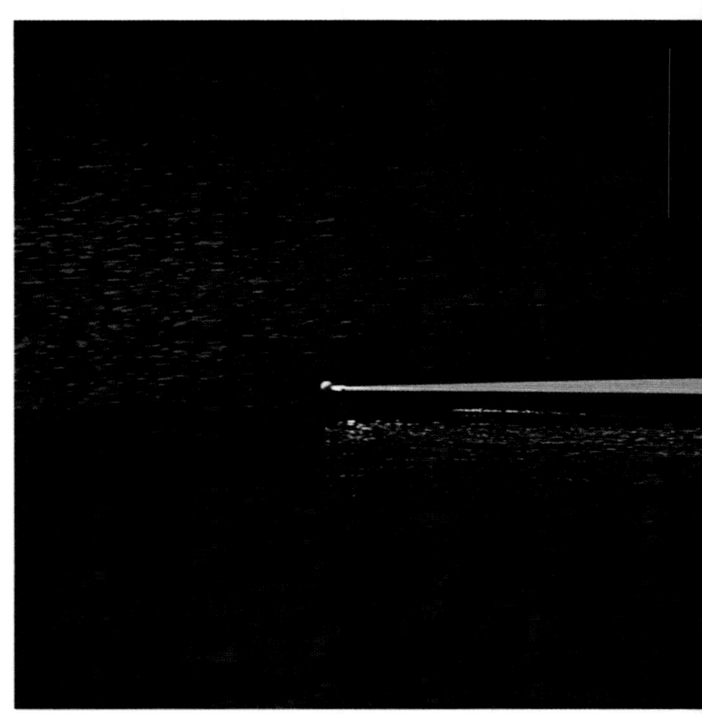

The Museum of Science and Industry is a place where everyone can spend an hour or a day viewing more enthrallments than can be listed.

These seasonal views of a willow in Lincoln Park make it hard for some to imagine that this park is in the middle of a booming metropolis. But Lincoln Park, like so many places in Chicago, offers a respite for citizens and visitors alike.

An early-morning view of a patch of Chicago skyline as seen from Navy Pier. The tall, curved building just to the right of center is Lake Point Tower.

Chicago Fire Department paramedics carry an unconscious diver near the Adler Planetarium.

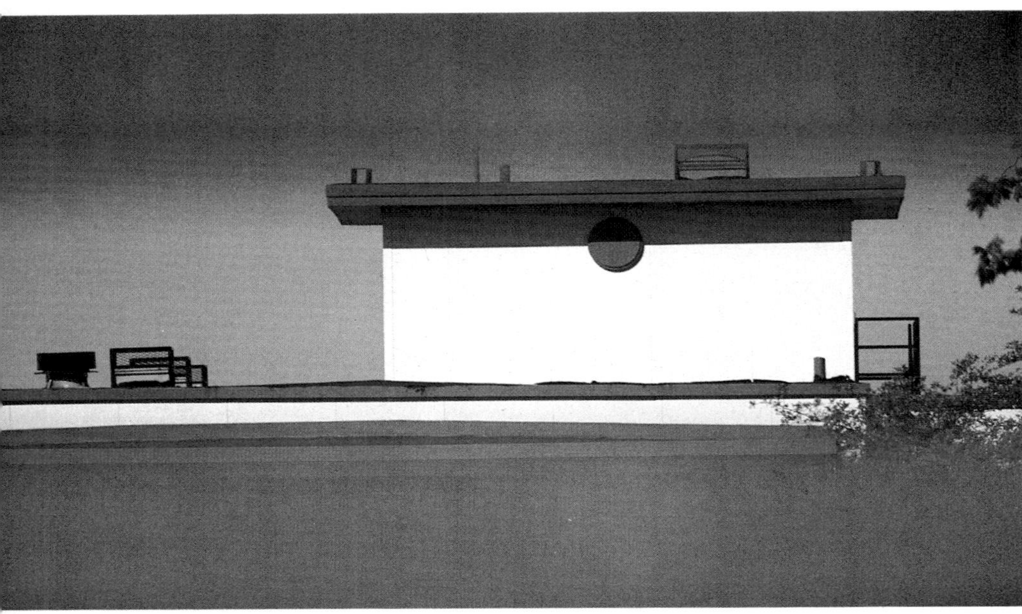

This view of a Lincoln Park beach house was shot between the rails of red fence.

The willows near the Lincoln Park lagoon are favorite haunts of many Chicagoans.

Lincoln Park is a great place to stroll regardless of the season, but it is especially inviting during autumn.

These chess players on North Avenue Beach idle the hours away challenging one another. Smelt fishers rise in the wee hours to try their luck in the unpredictable waters of Lake Michigan.

OPPOSITE
Fog shrouds the John Hancock Center, 900 North Michigan Avenue, and huddled buildings in mist, adding a curious beauty to the Lincoln Park lagoon, which records their inverted images.

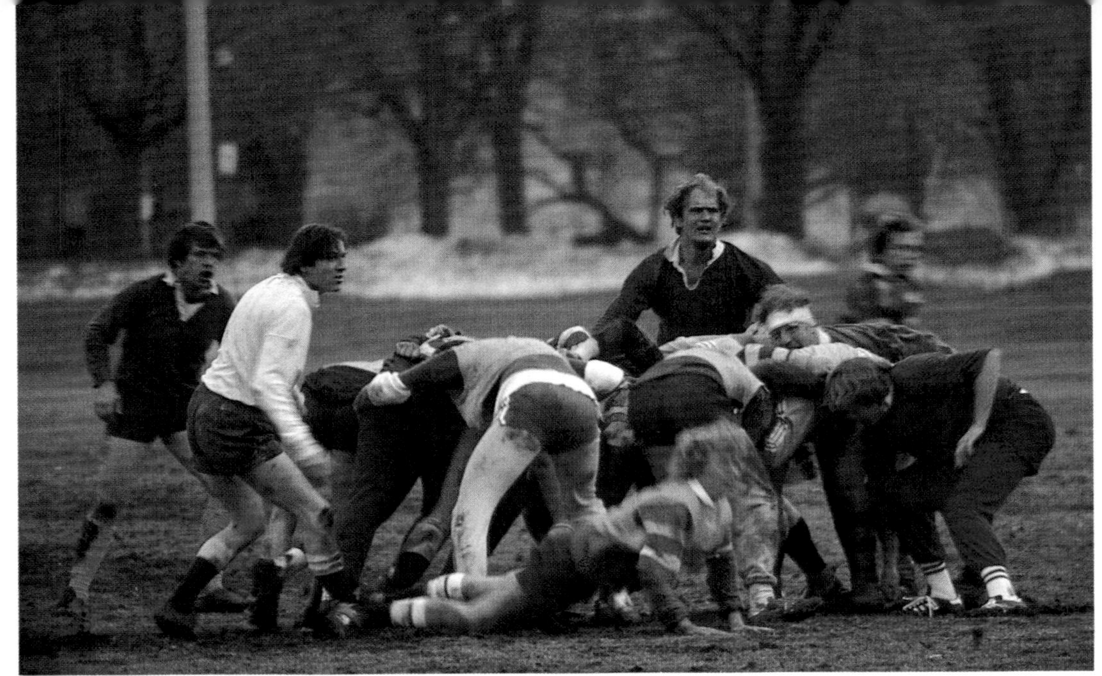

This is a sampling of the many pleasures available along Chicago's lakefront. It appeals to everyone, from rugby and basketball players, to anglers and balloon enthusiasts.

The movements may seem choreographed, but this picture captures the summertime mood of so many Chicago beaches. Here is the city's famed Oak Street Beach, with its sauntering passersby, freewheeling birds, and horizon-hugging sailboats.

Fulton Market is where trucks congregate at dawn to deliver meat, fish, eggs, and other foodstuffs to warehouses. About eight o'clock, frozen edibles arrive at the Fulton Cold Storage building, from whose roof this mini traffic jam is seen.

Chicago
CITY AT WORK

veryone knows that it is illegal to write about Chicago without quoting Carl Sandburg, poet and Lincoln biographer, who in 1916 had this to say about the town:

> Hog butcher for the world,
> Tool maker, stacker of wheat,
> Player with railroads
> and the nation's freight handler;
> Stormy, husky, brawling,
> City of the big shoulders.

Things have changed since then, because Chicago no longer is hog butcher for the world. But otherwise...

More than 58 million tons of manufactured goods—ranging from steel, sausages, and barrels to mattresses, machine tools, and surgical instruments—leave Chicago yearly by rail or truck, a figure no other production area in the nation can match. Less impressive figures can be offered for freight carried by ship or barge. If you'd like a more exotic statistic, about 200 large freighters from many ports and countries ply the St. Lawrence Seaway and Great Lakes to reach Chicago waters yearly.

Furthermore, only 15 countries in the world have gross national product figures greater than the Chicago area's gross metropolitan product—$174 billion, or about four percent of the GNP. And if we wanted to be boastful, we could name a number of products that Chicago makes more of than any other place in the country.

The city is uniquely situated for commerce, as early explorers appreciated. Via the Chicago, Des Plaines, and Illinois rivers, it is the link between shipping on the Great Lakes and river freight on the Mississippi. Steel mills in South Chicago and adjacent Gary and Hammond, Indiana, owed their existence to iron ore, coke, and coal shipped from other Great Lakes ports. Rail lines and highways converge on Chicago because of its location at the southern tip of Lake Michigan, which deflects more northerly traffic around it. And Chicago is a good stopping point between the East and the West.

Chicago has the world's tallest building (Sears Tower), as well as the fourth and fifth tallest (Amoco Oil and Hancock), the busiest airport (O'Hare International), the tallest apartment building (Lake Point Tower), the largest parking garage (O'Hare), the largest printing firm (R.R. Donnelley & Sons Company), and the greatest grain and futures markets. The Merchandise Mart is known as the world's largest commercial building, and until a few years ago the Conrad Hilton (now the Chicago Hilton and Towers) was known as the country's largest hotel, and the Chicago post office as the world's largest.

Twenty-five percent of the nation's people live within a 300-mile radius of Chicago, and thousands of them spend a lot of time flying in and out of O'Hare, which came into existence in 1946 with the closing of the Douglas Aircraft plant at that location.

O'Hare replaced Midway Airport in importance in 1961 and has been the world's busiest airport since that date, except when Saigon took the title during the Vietnam War. Some 45 major airlines use the field and in 1989 almost 800,000 flights were handled. On the average, a plane takes off or lands at the rate of two each minute, which ends up involving more than 53 million passengers and approximately 1,056,000 tons of mail or other cargo each year. Ten thousand cars can be parked in the airport's nine-story garage, plus thousands more in outdoor lots.

Two Chicago features that all out-of-towners seem to have heard about, and that even Chicagoans sometimes tend to sound superior about, are the Loop and that portion of Michigan Avenue known as the Magnificent Mile.

The Loop originally referred to the way in which the elevated tracks circled most of the downtown business district; now the term is usually used as an easy way of designating the business section itself. The Loop is a mixture of department stores, towering office buildings, hotels, restaurants, bookstores, and everything else you would expect to find in a big-city business center. It has motion-picture houses and legitimate theaters, although the movies shown today are perhaps not of the quality of those that used to have their premieres there. (Many of the top-quality films are now seen first in the outlying houses.) But the State Street Mall has added a pleasant new feeling to that famous thoroughfare and, while several of the well-known department stores now have suburban branches, their Loop establishments still draw both local and visiting customers.

The Magnificent Mile, just above the river, could be a penurious husband's nightmare, in view of the variety and elegance of the shops that it offers. Jewelry, gold and silver, clothing, footwear, art, books, and eating places of high distinction are only a small sampling of the enticements. The Tribune Tower, the Wrigley Building, the Equitable Building, Water Tower Place, the John Hancock Center, and other superb structures grace the Magnificent Mile, as do a number of first-class hotels, both old and new. In brief, there are enough shopping or browsing opportunities to keep a person busy for days. It is possible to step from the street into an almost-dream world at some points along the way. Ride the greenery-surrounded escalator to the heart of the grand atrium of the seven-floor vertical shopping center at Water Tower Place. See Chicago at your feet from the restaurant or the observation tower at the top of the John Hancock Center. Or enter the elegance of one of the last of the city's grand old hotels, the Drake.

There are scores of business firms in Chicago whose

This view was taken from the Tribune Tower's roof. There's the clock of the Wrigley Building. The Michigan Avenue Bridge is below, and ill-fated Fort Dearborn used to be just across the river. There's a portion of the westbound river, and in the distance, the Sears Tower.

local origins go back into the 19th century. Among these are two general department stores, Marshall Field's and Carson Pirie Scott; John M. Smyth Company (furniture); Lyon & Healy (musical instruments); Libby, McNeill and Libby (foodstuffs); Rand McNally (maps and publishing), although they later moved their headquarters building a short distance north of the city, leaving only a couple retail stores downtown; and the two pioneer mail-order firms, Montgomery Ward & Co. and Sears, Roebuck and Co. In addition there are firms in other categories, such as Brunswick Corporation (bowling and billiards equipment) and U.S. Gypsum (building materials), to fill out a most incomplete list.

Marshall Field, an Easterner who began his Chicago career as a clerk, was quiet spoken and perhaps the smartest merchant who ever welcomed a customer. By 1865 he was so successful that he gave up a partnership in another firm to join Levi Z. Leiter in acquiring control of Potter Palmer's drygoods business on Lake Street. When their prosperous new store was destroyed in the fire of 1871, Field and Leiter saved as much stock as they could and rented a warehouse in Valparaiso, Indiana, to hold goods ordered from the East until they could open their temporary store—a brick horse barn on the South Side.

They were back on State Street by the fall of 1873 but were burned out again four years later. Quality and an unfailing rule that the customers were right, even when they were wrong, had made the store highly successful. In fact, Field and Leiter were so successful that when they once again moved back to State Street from temporary quarters on the lakefront, they had the funds to purchase a new building that had been built on their old site.

In later life, even before he gave vast sums of money to found and then support the Columbian Museum, which became the Field Museum of Natural History, Field was known as a philanthropist, although never a careless one. He donated land and money to the University of Chicago, which was reborn in 1892, and to the Chicago Home for Incurables.

The present store, recently purchased from a British firm by a Minneapolis outfit, is one of the largest department stores found anywhere, with nine floors of merchandise. There are branches in Illinois, Texas, Wisconsin, Ohio, and Illinois, with 15,000 employees.

Carson Pirie Scott was founded in 1867 by Samuel Carson and John T. Pirie, who had owned stores elsewhere in Illinois before starting a wholesale drygoods business in Chicago in 1864. Two brothers, George and Robert Scott, and Andrew MacLeish also were partners. Their first store was on Lake Street, but the firm moved to State Street sometime after Field and Leiter shifted their business there. Carson's now owns 30-odd branch stores.

Two of the most spectacular success stories in the history of Chicago business are those of its two great mail-order houses. Aaron Montgomery Ward founded Montgomery Ward & Co. in 1872, using a borrowed $1,600 to open a 12-by-14-foot office on the 14th floor of 825 North Clark Street. His first catalog was a single sheet of paper describing 163 items. Ward himself wrote the early sales copy and was scrupulously careful to avoid false or extravagant claims. After one description of pots and pans he added this caveat: "Manufacturer's measure, will not hold quite as much as represented."

A money-back guarantee of customer satisfaction, which appeared in the 1875 catalog, is said to have been the first ever offered by a major merchandiser. Ward's also was the first to use fashion illustrations (1875) and photographs of live models (1878). In 1887, sales topped the million-dollar mark for the first time, and in 1888 the firm moved into its new building at Madison and Michigan avenues. The addition of a tower in 1899 and then of the statue of *Progress Lighting the Way for Commerce* in 1900 made the Ward Tower the tallest commercial building in the world at the time.

The company went into the retail store business in 1926, somewhat by accident. A carpenter in Plymouth, Indiana, admired a saw in one of the merchandise displays intended to drum up interest in the mail-order

catalog and insisted on buying it immediately. When he was allowed to do so, others demanded the right also to buy at once, and sales were so brisk that the retail store was born. Ward's sales exceeded $5 billion in 1978, 106 years after Ward rented that 12-by-14-foot office.

Only the most inept of Hollywood screenwriters would expect anyone to believe that the great firm of Sears, Roebuck and Co. began because someone sent a jeweler in Redwood Falls, Minnesota, a shipment of watches he had not ordered. But that is what happened. The watches arrived at the North Redwood railroad station in 1886, where a young man, Richard Sears, was agent and telegraph operator. When the jeweler refused to accept delivery, Sears bought the watches and quickly sold them, mostly to fellow agents up and down the line. He then ordered more, which he also sold readily.

Business became so good that Sears soon quit railroading and moved to Minneapolis, where he started a watch company. By 1887 he had shifted to Chicago, where he advertised for a watchmaker who had his own tools. Another young man, Alvah C. Roebuck, answered, impelled perhaps by the fact that he was making only $3.50 a week, plus room and board, in Hammond, Indiana. Sears hired him. When the watch company turned into a mail-order house in 1893, Sears made Roebuck a partner. Two years later, however, Roebuck sold his one-third interest in the company. Julius Rosenwald, who was to become one of the country's best-known philanthropists, bought into the firm.

The first catalog, in 1888, had offered only watches and jewelry. But the first general catalog went out in 1896, and the company's fortunes kept rising as dramatically as Ward's had. The huge new headquarters building and catalog distribution center opened on Chicago's West Side in 1906. Sears retired as president and was succeeded by Rosenwald in 1908. Eventually both Sears and Ward's had both retail and catalog stores scattered throughout this country and abroad. In 1945 Sears' total sales passed the billion-dollar mark. Today Sears is the world's largest general merchandising firm; its 1989 rev-

This water stream arcs over the river at intervals, partially concealing the Chicago Sun-Times *Building in the background.*

enues were $53.8 billion from all Sears businesses.

In 1974 Sears, Roebuck and Co. moved its corporate headquarters to the new Sears Tower. The 110-story building is 1,454 feet high, or 104 feet taller than its closest rival, the World Trade Center in New York City. The largest private office complex in the world (the Pentagon is larger), it has 4.5 million square feet of space, the equivalent of 100 acres. It took four years to build, even though at times there were 1,600 workers laboring simultaneously. The skydeck observation area on the 103rd floor is completely enclosed and affords breathtaking views of Chicagoland. The skydeck is reached by two express elevators which climb the 105 floors in less than one minute.

The merchandising group of Sears, a portion of the 7,000 Sears personnel currently in the Tower, is slated to move to a new 800-acre location in suburban Hoffman Estates sometime in 1992. Two hundred acres of the land will be utilized for the new headquarters.

The second tallest of Chicago's skyscrapers, at 200 East Randolph Drive, is corporate headquarters for the Amoco Corporation. It has only 80 stories but climbs to 1,136 feet, which gives it a nine-foot edge over the 110-story Hancock Center. The gleaming Amoco Tower (formerly the Standard Oil Building) was the world's largest marble-covered structure, with 43,000 slabs from Italy's Carrara Mountains, where Michelangelo obtained his marble some centuries ago. Now, however, the marble has been replaced by Mount Airy granite from North Carolina.

Edward Durell Stone's design includes an open-air plaza with honey locusts and a tremendous waterfall. Other features of the building, which has 51 floors reserved for Amoco offices, are five Swedish crystal chandeliers, each weighing one and a half tons, in the north and south lobbies, and the art collection, almost 7,000 pieces, by some 2,000 artists from 94 nations. These cover work done from the Renaissance to the present. About 2,000 of the pieces are by 400 or so Chicago-area artists.

Eight bronze busts stand near the main entrance to the Merchandise Mart. They honor pioneer retail merchants who made major contributions to the nation's economic welfare.

The Hancock Center, which upon completion was promptly nicknamed "Big John" by a *Chicago Daily News* writer, is on Michigan Avenue about two blocks north of the old Water Tower. It was the first Chicago skyscraper to surpass 1,000 feet and was second only to New York's Empire State Building when completed. The Hancock is now fifth on the world's tallest list and the Empire State is third.

The Hancock Center, which has a base of 47,000 square feet, tapers upward to a top of only 16,000 square feet. It is said to be one of the world's tallest office-and-residential buildings, with offices from the 13th to 41st floors and about 700 apartment condominiums, ranging from efficiency to four-bedroom, on the 45th to 92d floors. The Hancock has a commissary, indoor swimming pool, health club, restaurant, and specialty shops for residents. There are also public restaurants and other amenities, including an observation floor, for visitors. A cluster of antennas serves local television, radio, and data-transmitting stations.

This may sound like boasting, but Chicago seems to have more fascinating buildings than is fair to the rest of the country. The Merchandise Mart, which sprawls along the river a bit west of those conversation pieces, the Marina Towers, is a case in point.

This 25-story giant, which has seven and a half miles of corridors and covers space enough for a couple of city blocks, was built by Marshall Field & Company at a cost of $32 million and opened May 1, 1930. The building was sold to Joseph P. Kennedy in 1945. The Kennedy family still owns the complex.

The Mart Center also includes the Apparel Center, which houses Expocenter/Chicago, and has a combined area of 650,000 square feet. The Apparel Center, opened in 1977, serves as a showplace for some 4,000 lines of clothing and accessories. It has a 550-room hotel in the top 10 floors of one of its twin towers.

The Mart is the world's largest commercial building, with more square footage (4.2 million) than *any* other building except the Pentagon. Two major reconstruction

These shoeshiners at Michigan and Chicago earn extra bucks while the sailors make sure their footgear is shipshape.

This nurse tends a two-day-old premature infant born at Mt. Sinai Hospital Medical Center. This is one of several research institutions that make Chicago a leader in the medical field.

projects are under way: The first, to cost $50 million, will fashion a retail shopping mall on the first two floors, accommodating 85 tenants, among them Carson Pirie Scott and The Limited. According to Philip E. Kelley, Mart president, the new mall will put the River North area on a par with State Street or North Michigan Avenue. The mall will open by the summer of 1991.

The other improvement ($100 million) won't be done until 1994. It calls for cleaning the entire white limestone facade, a new roof, replacing 4,000 windows, improving the elevators, adding five new entrances, making a new atrium, and upgrading the heating, cooling, and plumbing. Other mall tenants will be a varied lot: three restaurants, and purveyors of such merchandise as books, eyeglasses, toys, tapes, records, etc. The top floors will continue to be occupied by wholesale showrooms and offices.

A covered pedestrian bridge will link the Mart and the Apparel Center, and combined square footage will be approximately 6 million. About 9,000 persons work in the Mart and Apparel Center. The Mart's major tenant, the National Broadcasting Company, recently moved into its own building at 454 North Columbus Drive.

Over the river and south several blocks is Chicago's financial district, concentrated on LaSalle Street—a mélange of giant banks with billions of dollars in assets; brokerage houses; law firms; and exchanges, including the new Chicago Board of Options Exchange, the world's central marketplace for stock-option trading. The Exchange is housed in the Chicago Board of Trade Building at the foot of LaSalle Street, which opened in 1930 just after the stock market crash. This was about the 13th move for the Chicago Board of Trade, which was organized in 1848. A 23-story addition behind the main structure was completed a few years ago, enlarging the total trading area—which spans three floors—to 55,000 square feet. Some 250,000 contracts worth billions of dollars are bought and sold here every day.

The Board of Trade is a futures market; very few of the items purchased ever are seen by the buyer. Sellers include the owners of grain elevators, where huge quantities are in storage. These business people sell futures contracts at the time they purchase grain in order to insure themselves against a subsequent drop in price, which could be disastrous without this hedge. A drop of one cent per bushel, for example, would mean a $100,000 loss on a million bushels. Among the buyers of futures contracts are flour millers, bakers, and cereal manufacturers, who need to protect themselves against price rises of their raw material. Many other buyers are speculators, of course, betting that prices will either drop or increase at some future date. The risks are substantial, but so are the possible profits. We know one trader who guessed right on soybeans and was able to quit the Board

Continued on page 83.

No longer molten, but very definitely red hot, steel is coming off the billet-caster at Inland Steel Company's Indiana Harbor plant. The billets are cooled and cut, then shipped to a bar mill, where they are melted once more and shaped for sale. Inland is one of Chicagoland's oldest companies.

Escalators at Water Tower Place, decorated for the Christmas season, carry patrons throughout this seven-level shopping emporium.

FOLLOWING PAGE
Homebound pedestrians trudging through the slush on their way across the Michigan Avenue Bridge probably would not argue with a 300-year-old conclusion by George Herbert, who said, "Every mile is two in winter."

FLY

A lazy summer day on the Chicago River means these water craft can go about their business at any pace. For the tugboat, it means towing; for the smaller motorized boats, it means pleasure cruising.

OPPOSITE
The Merchandise Mart was built for $32 million and is being refurbished for several times that amount. The Mart, once a headquarters for wholesale trade, will also have a number of excellent retail stores.

Two mounted police officers have the pleasant task of patrolling the lakefront on a blustery Chicago day.

This raised railroad bridge obligingly permits a clear look at the Sears Tower, the world's highest skyscraper, from an unusual angle.

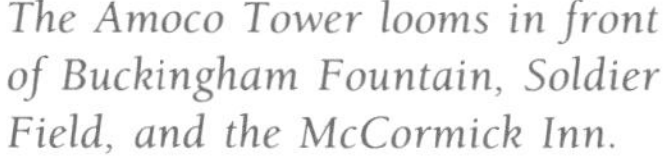

The Amoco Tower looms in front of Buckingham Fountain, Soldier Field, and the McCormick Inn.

of Trade and fulfill an old dream. He became an architect.

Chicago industry is not all manufacturing, sales, and finance. Chicago long has been a major publishing center. It is the home, for example, of the *Encyclopaedia Britannica,* which recently issued its 15th edition. First published in Scotland in 1768, the *Britannica* is the oldest continuously published reference work in the English language. Eventually it became a joint English-American venture, which Julius Rosenwald of Sears, Roebuck and Co. bought in 1920. The *Encyclopaedia Britannica,* which also publishes *Compton's Encyclopedia* and other works, is owned by the William Benton Foundation of Illinois, which makes substantial grants to the University of Chicago.

Chicago has given birth to major magazines, including *Esquire, Popular Mechanics,* and *Science Digest*—all of which moved to the East; *Playboy,* which continues to flourish here; Harriet Monroe's *Poetry;* the excellent *Chicago,* which grows fatter and fatter; and a comparative newcomer, the *Chicago Times.*

The nation's leading magazine for blacks, *Ebony,* is published in Chicago by the Johnson Publishing Company, Inc., which also publishes two others, *Jet* and *Ebony Man.* In 1942 John Harold Johnson, then a 24-year-old, $25-a-month office boy, launched his first magazine, *Negro Digest,* with a $500 loan he obtained using his mother's furniture as collateral. Three years later, *Ebony* hit the stands. The new magazine was an overnight success and now has a circulation of 1,800,000 and worldwide distribution. Today the Johnson Publishing Company, Inc., housed in its own $7 million, 11-story building at 820 South Michigan Avenue, is the second largest black-owned nonfinancial company in the nation. The *Ebony* staff includes Lerone Bennett, an authority on black history.

The City of the Big Shoulders has grown huskier since Sandburg's day, in the process of becoming a bit less stormy and brawling. But Chicago is still a place where big things happen every day. Chicagoans absorb a feeling of strength from their city, a strength arising, at least in part, from its solid industries and its thriving marketplaces.

When Montgomery Ward built a new administration building at 615 West Chicago in 1928, George Mulligan's Spirit of Progress *went on top.*

Marshall Field's is bright with Christmas decorations, but this youngster seems more interested in his out-of-season milkshake. He also doesn't seem to mind the snow; however, the plodding pedestrians heading past the giant tree in Daley Center Plaza near the Cook County building probably do.

On the job at sunrise: This shot of a distant Loop building under construction was taken from Halsted and Hubbard.

Divers at the Shedd Aquarium feed the Coral Reef population twice daily and three times on weekends. This tank measures 40 feet across and holds 90,000 gallons of sea water.

On the left are the Chicago Board of Trade and the Chicago Board Options Exchange, both on LaSalle Street in the heart of Chicago's financial district. The statue on top of the Board of Trade is Ceres, Roman goddess of agriculture.

These folks are buying and selling options in the grain pits, which are very lucrative or very depressing. A drop of one cent per bushel, for example, would mean a $100,000 loss on a million bushels.

FOLLOWING PAGE
Industrial area near the International Port of Chicago, where ships from around the world end their journeys. Chicago is one of the world's largest inland seaports. About 200 ships arrive yearly from 42 foreign countries.

Nº16

All vistas seem to zero in on the Sears Tower, which motorists coming south on the Kennedy Expressway can see until they duck into Hubbard's Cave. This underground stretch of the expressway, a rush-hour traffic bottleneck, has an eerie orange glow due to its lighting and reflective walls.

Bridge over the muddy Calumet River, one of many waterways linking Chicago's industries to the rest of the world.

Any lunch seems more appetizing if eaten while gazing at a Marc Chagall mosaic. This example of the artist's work is in the First Chicago Plaza.

Chicago

CITY OF ARTS & SPORTS

Snow and city lights add a slightly demonic look to the Picasso, which is slowly becoming a Chicago totem. This massive sculpture stands in Daley Center Plaza near City Hall.

Perhaps because of the faint but lingering echo of gangland guns or the distracting roar of jet planes, too many persons have forgotten that Chicago has played a major role in the various arts during the last century.

Chicago has one of the best art museums to be found anywhere, with an enviable collection of French Impressionists and a wealth of other treasures; it has breathtaking sculptures in Loop plazas and buildings, created by such international greats as Picasso, Chagall, and Calder; it has a symphony orchestra that most critics agree is unrivaled; and there is the Lyric Opera of Chicago, which for years has sold out virtually every performance. Chicago citizens, both the native-born and adopted, are prominent on any roster of famous writers. Architects around the world know Chicago as the cradle of the skyscraper, a showplace of modern architecture, and the home of such architectural greats as Louis Sullivan, Frank Lloyd Wright, and Ludwig Mies van der Rohe. And Chicago, with its world-famous universities, institutes, and professional schools, is a center of learning.

The Art Institute of Chicago has developed into an exceptional museum in the years since various wealthy Chicagoans were persuaded to finance its birth. The first of its many exhibitions was held in 1885, eight years before the building it now occupies on South Michigan Avenue was completed. While the most famous of its collections may well be that of the Impressionists, the museum's various acquisitions have given it a well-balanced look.

Even before the 20th century began, generous Chicagoans had donated to the young museum a small but choice group of Dutch and Flemish paintings. Among them were works by Meindert Hobbema and Jan Steen, as well as Rembrandt's charming *Young Girl at an Open Half-Door*.

Only a few of the varied objects now housed in the Art Institute can be mentioned here, but the museum suggests a dozen of the choicest things for first-time visitors to see: a T'ang dynasty horse; a painted altarpiece from 12th century Spain; El Greco's *The Assumption of the Virgin;* Rembrandt's *Young Girl; On the Terrace,* by Renoir; Gustave Caillebotte's *Paris, a Rainy Day;* Cezanne's *The Basket of Apples;* Seurat's *Sunday Afternoon on the Island of La Grande Jatte; Portrait of Daniel-Henry Kahnweiler,* by Picasso; Grant Wood's *American Gothic;* Mary Cassatt's *The Bath;* and the three stained-glass windows installed in 1977 by the French master Marc Chagall.

Two bronze lions outside the museum are Chicago landmarks. Designed by Edward L. Kemeys and donated by Mrs. Henry Field, each lion weighs about three tons, and neither seems at all upset by the number of youngsters who climb onto its back every year.

The museum has 10 curatorial departments, providing enough variety to satisfy even the most eclectic tastes. These comprise: European paintings; 20th century paintings and sculpture; American arts, including furniture, silver, glass, and ceramics from the 17th century to date; European decorative arts and sculpture; textiles; prints; architecture; photography (heavy on Alfred Stieglitz, Edward Weston, Paul Strand, Eugene Atget, and Andre Kertesz and including William Henry Fox Talbot, Julia Cameron and others); Oriental and classical art; and ceramics from Africa, America, and Oceania. The total collections number over 250,000 art objects, which explains why a recent addition to the Institute was mandatory.

It should be added that the Institute's school offers training and degrees in various artistic areas.

Strictly modern and often startling works are displayed a mile north of the Art Institute at the Museum of Contemporary Art, 237 East Ontario Street. The largest permanent exhibit in the place is a sound sculpture by Max Neuhaus in the west wing stairwell. Otherwise you may view an ever-changing selection of paintings, sculpture, photographs, graphics, and other art forms.

One of the newest of the town's general-interest museums is the Terra Museum of American Art, which opened in April, 1987, at North Michigan Avenue and Erie Street. The museum began in Evanston with the private collection of Daniel J. Terra, cultural ambassador-at-large during the presidency of Ronald Reagan. The most famous painting on display is *Gallery of the Louvre,* by Samuel Morse, inventor of the telegraph, who was an artist and early photographer. The permanent collection also includes work by Winslow Homer, John Singer Sargent, James A.M. Whistler, Andrew Wyeth, Mary Cassatt, and Edward Hopper. The museum displays traveling shows from various galleries and drew 5,000 viewers during one year-end holiday period.

The Chicago Symphony Orchestra is the third oldest such group in the nation. It was founded in 1891 by Theodore Thomas, a concert violinist and conductor who, incidentally, was in town with his own touring orchestra in the autumn of 1871 and was upstaged by the Great Fire. The Chicago Symphony moved from the Auditorium Theater, Louis Sullivan's architectural triumph, to Orchestra Hall in December, 1904, less than a month before Thomas died. Frederick Stock became director and remained in that post until his death in 1942.

A succession of directors followed, until Sir Georg Solti, a native of Hungary, took up the baton in 1969. When Solti and the Chicago went east a few months later, an enthusiastic Carnegie Hall audience stood and applauded for 10 tumultuous minutes, and a reviewer wrote that "nobody wanted to leave. Even the critics

lingered, the ultimate test."

In 1971 Sir Georg and the orchestra, with Carlo Maria Giulini as principal guest conductor (1969-73), made their first international appearance. Critics in 15 cities and nine European countries joined with the crowds that turned out in hailing a series of brilliant performances. Solti and the Chicago returned to Europe in 1974, visited Japan in 1977, and again went to Europe in 1978. Critics in almost a dozen countries hunted for new superlatives:

> LONDON— "Nobody could doubt that this is about the most formidably equipped orchestra in the world at present." (*The Times*)
>
> BRUSSELS— "And what an orchestra! Not a single failing." (*Le Travail*)
>
> VIENNA— "The technical quality of the ensemble is phenomenal." (*Kurier*)
>
> PARIS— "Musical perfection exists in the world." (*L'Aurore*)
>
> JAPAN— "Here we have continuous rich feasting. Breakfast at Tiffany's, lunch at Cartier's, and dinner at Harry Winston's." (*Daily Yomiuri*)

Irving Lowens, of the *Washington Star,* spoke the definitive word: "Let's lay it on the line. Under Sir Georg Solti, something has happened, and the Chicagoans have become the world's greatest orchestra, bar none....Today, the Chicago Symphony Orchestra is the pacemaker. One measures the rest of the world's orchestras by how they compare to the Chicago."

Sir Georg steps down as music director in 1991 to become music director laureate. In the 1991-1992 season, Daniel Barenboim becomes music director of the Chicago Symphony Orchestra.

There were many opera seasons in Chicago before the first resident company began in 1910. One of the highlights of the 1889 season was the dedication of that acoustical marvel the Auditorium Theater, during which the celebrated Adelina Patti, though well past her prime as a singer, delighted the audience with a moving rendition of "Home Sweet Home."

After the Chicago Opera Company was formed in 1910 it very quickly obtained some priceless, if unwanted publicity. Mary Garden, one of the great prima donnas, forced the early closing of *Salome* when she played the title role with a sensual conviction that upset some of the more inhibited members of the audience. Miss Garden later directed the company, during the 1921 season.

Chicago resident opera companies continued through 1946, then there was an eight-year hiatus, ending when the Lyric Theatre was founded by Carol Fox, a trained singer and opera enthusiast; Lawrence Kelly, Chicago businessman and opera lover; and Nicola Recigno, noted opera conductor.

Maria Callas made her American debut during the Lyric's 1954 season. The group reorganized as the Lyric Opera in 1956, and since has staged more than 130 different operas. It also has enjoyed tremendous community support, reaching a new level in 1990, when the entire season sold out months before it began, a phenomenon which, it is believed, no other opera company in this country or Europe ever has enjoyed.

This huge sundial, beautifully silhouetted against a sunless sky near Adler Planetarium, needs this passing pedestrian to give some idea of its dimension. The Henry Moore creation is but one example of Chicago's fantastic art and architecture.

In 1958 the Lyric's international reputation was spotlighted when the Italian government gave it a $16,000 grant. Pleasantly enough, the Lyric was able to respond in 1966 by raising $15,000 for Italian flood relief, and again a few years ago when it sent $200,000 to aid Italian earthquake victims.

Ardis Krainik is general director of the Lyric, and Bruno Bartoletti has been artistic director for a quarter of a century.

Literature is an area in which Chicago has been so well represented that it would be presumptuous and certainly foolhardy to try to compile any complete roster of names-to-remember. A kind of butterfly look at the literary scene is about all that can be attempted.

It is difficult to say what created the ambience that persuaded so many native or born-elsewhere Chicagoans to become writers. But some of the ingredients are known. One certainly was the Whitechapel Club, which later merged with the Chicago Press Club. Opie Read, who signed his humorous writings "The Arkansas Traveler," is credited with founding the Whitechapel. Its president was a writer of biography, with a magnificent name: Hobart Chatfield Chatfield-Taylor. Other noted members were Finley Peter Dunne (Mr. Dooley); Eugene Field, who wrote some very popular verses for young people, including "Little Boy Blue"; George Ade, humorist and playwright; and even a magician named Herman the Great.

A more basic factor was the *Chicago Daily News,* which attracted fine writers as if by some kind of magic. Field and Ade wrote for the *Daily News,* as eventually did Ben Hecht and Charles MacArthur. (He married Helen Hayes and with Hecht co-authored that great newspaper comedy *The Front Page,* which is a staple of late-night television.)

Others who helped make the *Daily News* famous as a breeding ground for writers were Harry Hansen, the book critic; Carl Sandburg, Lincoln biographer and poet; Vincent Starrett, who fashioned excellent light verse, wrote mysteries, and became the world's finest authority on Sherlock Holmes; foreign correspondent and author John Gunther; and Henry Sell, the paper's first book review editor. Columnist Mike Royko, now with the *Chicago Tribune,* gained his national following while writing for the *Daily News* and the *Chicago Sun-Times.* Royko went to the *Tribune* when the *Sun-Times* was bought by Rupert Murdoch, the controversial Australian press lord.

At the *Tribune* in the early days the number of outstanding writers may have been smaller, but the quality was there: sportswriter Ring Lardner; columnist Westbrook Pegler, before he was "bitten by an income tax"; William L. Shirer, foreign correspondent who later wrote *The Rise and Fall of the Third Reich;* Fanny Butcher, the literary critic for 50 years; and music and drama critic Claudia Cassidy, who still writes as beautifully as ever.

You can't talk about persons who make a town lively and conscious of things of the spirit without including the political cartoonists, at least not when they're as gifted as Chicago's have been during the last few decades. Consider the late John T. McCutcheon, remembered also for his nostalgic "Injun Summer"; other *Tribune* folk such as Carey Orr, Joe Parrish, Wayne Stayskal, Dick Locher, and Jeff MacNelly, formerly of the *Richmond News-Leader.* He has won three Pulitzer prizes, and Locher, McCutcheon, and Orr one each. Then there were Vaughn Shoemaker (two Pulitzers) and Cecil Jensen of the old *Daily News;* Bill Mauldin, John Fischetti, and Jacob Burck of the *Sun-Times* all won Pulitzers, with Mauldin, who created the sardonic GIs Willie and Joe during World War II, getting it twice. Nor should Chester Commodore of the *Chicago Daily Defender* be forgotten. He now lives in Colorado.

The town was alive with talent late into the 19th century and well into the 20th. Sherwood Anderson was around, as were Hendrik Willem Van Loon and Theodore Dreiser. Add to the list the poets Lew Sarrett, Edgar Lee Masters, and part-time Chicagoan Edna St. Vincent Millay.

The *Chicago Evening Post* could boast of Floyd Dell and Francis Hackett. Elsewhere were Edna Ferber; Upton Sinclair, who won a Pulitzer with *Dragon's Teeth* but much more fame with *The Jungle;* William Vaughn Moody; and so many more, all of them ghosts now.

Later, Thornton Wilder and Daniel Boorstin, both of whom taught at the University of Chicago, as well as Ernest Hemingway and Archibald MacLeish, would win Pulitzers. Wilder won three of the coveted awards—one for his novel *The Bridge of San Luis Ray* and one each for *Our Town* and *The Skin of Our Teeth.*

Chicago novelists who took their material from what went on in the neighborhood streets include James Farrell, who did a trilogy about a character named Studs Lonigan, from whom one of Chicago's best-known writers, Studs Terkel, took his nickname. Jack Conroy wrote *The Disinherited,* perhaps the earliest proletarian novel. The late Meyer Levin, who wrote *The Old Bunch,* became a resident of Israel but got back to his old haunts once in a while. Nelson Algren (*A Walk on the Wild Side* and *The Man with the Golden Arm*) moved east, as so many of his predecessors did, and died, you might say, in exile. Harry Mark Petrakis, whose father was a Greek Orthodox priest on the city's South Side, still mines the Greek-American lode with great success, as in *A Dream of Kings,* later made into a movie.

Willard Motley, one of many fine black writers, wrote *Knock on Any Door* and *We Fished All Night.* Motley died in Mexico. Black novelist Richard Wright, most famous for *Native Son,* lived and wrote for many years in Chicago. So did the late Frank London Brown, author of *Trumbull Park.* Noted black women writers of Chicago include Pulitzer Prize-winning Gwendolyn Brooks, poet laureate of Illinois; the late Lorraine Hansberry, playwright of the poignant *A Raisin in the Sun,* and Era Bell Thompson, who died a few years ago.

Chicago's leading literary light today, without question, is Saul Bellow, who grew up here and teaches at the University of Chicago. In 1976 he won both the Pulitzer Prize, for his novel *Humboldt's Gift,* and the Nobel Prize in literature.

A very entertaining book, *Chicago's Left Bank,* by Alson J. Smith, has a more detailed account of the early Chicago writers and the so-called Chicago Renaissance following World War I. Smith also tells how jazz came up from New Orleans to make Chicago the "jazz capital of the world" for some 20 years. For a while Chicago was host to such musicians as "King" Joe Oliver; Louis Armstrong; Johnny and Baby Dodds; Eddie Condon; Bix Beiderbecke, who drifted in from Davenport, Iowa; Fats Waller; Art Hodes, a classy piano player who's still

Bits of two great universities: the open-air Forum on the spacious University of Illinois at Chicago campus and Rockefeller Memorial Chapel at the University of Chicago. A large gift from John D. Rockefeller enabled the latter university to open in 1812.

OPPOSITE
Henry Moore, for many years the most important figure in the British art world, created Nuclear Energy, *the bronze sculpture on the University of Chicago campus near the spot where the first nuclear chain reaction occurred.*

Chicago boasts many private art collections. Most of this one consists of work by Chicago artists.

around; Earl (Fatha) Hines; Muggsy Spanier; and dozens more, among them the pianist Lil Hardin, who became the first Mrs. Louis Armstrong.

Lil, incidentally, never lost her touch. About 15 or 20 years ago, when someone threw a party for Willard Motley in a hall above a South Side bowling alley, Lil was asked to play. She tested the battered piano and discovered that several of the keys (six or seven, if memory serves) were stuck. But she played very beautifully and, when asked later how she dealt with the sticking-key problem, replied with cheerful assurance, "I just jumped over 'em."

Gene Krupa, Dave Tough, Dick McPartland, and Benny Goodman were among the native Chicagoans who went on to greatness in the music world. And a young fellow named Jules Herbuveaux, who played saxophone and had his own band, opened the Empire Room in the Palmer House on New Year's Eve some 50 years ago. Benny Goodman once played in Jules' band, and Jules, who later became an NBC vice-president, would tell you endless, and always engrossing, tales of what it was like on the Chicago music scene half a century ago.

Gospel singer Mahalia Jackson must be remembered when you talk about music in Chicago, and that memorable blues singer Etta Moten. She still adorns Chicago. Then there was the ever-sparkling Bricktop, who began singing the blues in Chicago, went to Paris, where she became famous, and returned to this country many years later to hear her hometown still applauding. Another of the old-time blues singers also was still here until some time ago—Howlin' Wolf (Chester Burnett), whom the Rolling Stones visited while in town because they said they owed so much to his example.

Chicago has long been known as a gathering and flowering place for folksingers and guitar and banjo players, largely because of the Old Town School of Folk Music, 909 West Armitage, founded in 1957 by Win Stracke, noted folksinger and actor. Graduates include such familiar names as Bonnie Kolac, John Prine, and the late Steve Goodman, among others. But in recent years the focus has widened to take in music and dance indigenous to many countries. The school now brings in musicians from Ireland, Africa, Eastern Europe, and the Latin nations and also has programs on African and Cajun dances.

Guitar and banjo are taught, but so are piano, flute, and other folk and classical instruments, and a successful effort has been made to gain the interest of the young. Of the thousand or so students who show up each week, about 350 are youngsters. Michael Miles, assistant director of the school, is especially pleased with the "wiggleworm" class attended by toddlers (and their parents) at which musical games are played and there is lots of laughter and fun. In fact, the Old Town School appeals to all ages. One student is in his 70s, and there is a six-month-old. He, needless to say, is a wiggle-worm.

Other Chicago cultural assets include WTTW-TV, the most-watched public television station in the nation, and radio station WFMT, which the *Chicago Tribune* bought and gave to WTTW. The late Herman Kogan, coauthor with Lloyd Wendt of five books of Chicago history and biography, as well as other works, had a highly popular interview show on WFMT, and was a former *Chicago Sun-Times* book editor. Louis (Studs) Terkel, who has written several best-sellers about various aspects of contemporary life, also is known across the land

The delicate traceries of Louis Henry Sullivan beautify the entrance to Carson Pirie Scott's Loop store. Although Sullivan left his fingerprints all over town, he died penniless.

as a superb on-air interviewer, and has been hosting such a show for WFMT for 36 years. Long ago Terkel had an early and smashingly popular television show, "Studs' Place," which also starred Bev Younger, Win Stracke, and Chet Roble.

WTTW (the call letters stand for "Window to the World") sends out 9,700 programs yearly, which are seen for about a 90-mile radius from the Sears Tower. Ten of the shows originate locally; others are imported from as far away as the BBC. The station is on the air 20 hours daily, seven days a week, again a record for a public broadcasting station. WTTW, which owes much of its success to the promotional efforts of a pair of civic-minded Chicagoans—the late Edward L. Ryerson and attorney Newton N. Minow—spends more than $30 million yearly to maintain the quality of its telecasts. The station went on the air in 1955 at the Museum of Science and Industry and moved to its present built-for-television structure on North St. Louis Avenue in 1965. Bill McCarter is the station director.

For a combination museum and research center it is hard to surpass the Chicago Historical Society on Clark Street at North Avenue. It is one of the largest such museums in the country, founded in 1856 and erased (briefly) by the Great Chicago Fire. Any right-thinking students of American history would be happy to bring their lunch and never again leave the building. Its major collections range from the World's Columbian Exposition (1893) to Chicago crime, and it has marvelous dioramas and impressive gatherings of maps, broadsides, music, books, manuscripts, and other original documents, including a signed copy of the Thirteenth Amendment.

Lincoln's life mask is there, and the table on which Gen. Robert E. Lee signed the surrender at Appomattox. There also are Chicago Fire artifacts and a very convincing recreation of that holocaust. The rooms furnished in 19th century style captivate visitors, of whom there are more than 200,000 yearly. A recent three-story addition provides space for a fine photography collection and a temperature-and-humidity-controlled area for many exhibits. The late Paul Angle, a noted Lincoln scholar, was the director for many years. He was succeeded by Ellsworth Brown.

National pride has led to the founding of several ethnic museums well worth visiting, depending upon your interests. Typically, each includes paintings, sculptures, objects of religious and/or historic interest, and a sizable library. Thus, there are the DuSable Museum of African-American History at 740 East 56th Place; the Maurice Spertus Museum of Judaica at 618 South Michigan Avenue; the Balzekas Museum of Lithuanian Culture, 4012 South Archer Avenue; and the Polish Museum of America at 984 North Milwaukee Avenue.

One of the greatest research libraries in the world is the Newberry. Located off Clark Street, a few blocks south of the Historical Society, the Newberry Library was established almost by chance. Chicago banker Walter Loomis Newberry, father of two young and attractive daughters, had provided in his will for the establishment of such a library—after his wife's death and only if his daughters had no children. Then, in poor health himself, he left for France by ship in 1868.

Newberry died before reaching Le Havre. One daughter, Mary, died in southern France in 1874, and Julia, the other daughter, in Rome two years later. When Newberry's widow, another Julia, followed them in 1885, the sum of $2,150,000 became available to start the library.

Scholars from across the world come to Chicago to utilize the general research material as well as the special collections. The Newberry has some 1,400,000 books; 60,000 maps; 1,057,000 pieces of sheet music and manuscripts, with materials dating back to the Renaissance. Other areas covered are Western Americana and the histories of Brazil and Portugal, to name only a few. Charles Cullen is president and librarian.

Another fine institution, the Chicago Public Library, is scheduled to move into new quarters sometime in 1991 when its 10-story, $145 million building is completed on State Street between Van Buren and Congress. The library, with 82 branches, now owns a collection of 5 million books and has begun building its store of manuscripts, tapes, motion-picture films, recordings, and other material, including aids for bibliographical and genealogical research. Until it moves, the library has temporary headquarters at 400 North Franklin Street, while the Cultural Center, where the concentration is on art, music, and literature, remains, for the moment, in the old (1897) building at 78 East Washington.

Chicago's fame as a world mecca of modern architecture is either unknown or taken for granted by most Chicagoans. Few know that the Great Fire of 1871 thrust Chicago into this position. The fire utterly destroyed Chicago's business district, wiping the slate clean for rebuilding and creating a need so enormous that it could only be satisfied by builders and architects attracted to Chicago from all over the country. The need was not for ornate structures but for height, light, economy—met by no-nonsense buildings that were the hallmark of what came to be known as the Chicago School of Architecture (and later, as the first Chicago School of Architecture). The members of this elite group were engineers first of all and architects incidentally, who learned to replace masonry with iron and steel and glass.

The year before the fire, a Chicagoan, C.W. Baldwin, had invented the mechanical (hydraulic) elevator, which in turn made tall buildings feasible. Chicago's William Le Baron Jenney in 1884 created the world's first skeleton steel-and-iron building (the Home Insurance Building at 135 South LaSalle Street, demolished in 1931) which was the forerunner of all skyscrapers. (His 16-story Manhattan Building at 431 South Dearborn, built in 1890, is the oldest tall all-skeletal office building extant.) The 16-story Monadnock Building at 53 West Jackson, the largest office building in the world when it was built, crystallized the architectural revolution in midswing. The north half, built in 1891 by traditionalists Daniel H. Burnham and John Wellborn Root, was and still is the highest commercial building in the world with outside load-bearing walls; at the base they are six feet thick. The south half, built two years later by William Holabird and Martin Roche, is steel frame throughout.

Chicago's moist and uncertain soil led to another Chicago architectural innovation, the hollow caisson "floating foundation," developed by William Sooy Smith and Dankmar Adler. Adler and Louis Sullivan used it to support the Auditorium Building at 430 South Michigan, a marriage of engineering ingenuity and architectural artistry. Today the building houses Roosevelt University and the restored Auditorium Theater, as acoustically perfect and ornately beautiful as when Louis Sullivan designed it in 1889.

Sullivan's art at its finest is displayed in the Carson Pirie Scott building at State and Madison, with its broad windows and clean lines ornamented by delicate leaves and flowers of wrought iron. The architectural landmarks of Sullivan, who died a penniless alcoholic in 1924, are all over town, but he is almost as well known for another accomplishment. He launched the career of an even more famous architect, Frank Lloyd Wright, who began work as an $8-a-week draftsman for Adler and Sullivan in 1887, and in 1895 opened his own studio in the Chicago suburb of Oak Park. From the beginning, he was innovative.

Wright once suggested the feasibility of a mile-high building but is remembered principally for his graceful and airy designs, his use of native materials, and the development of the "Prairie House"—a house, which, in Wright's words, has "gently sloping roofs, low proportions, quiet sky lines, suppressed heavy-set chimneys and sheltering overhangs, low terraces and out-reaching walls sequestering private gardens." Although most of Wright's Prairie Houses were built in Oak Park, a notable example in Chicago is the Frederick C. Robie House (1909) at

Continued on page 121.

PASS
OTOS
TAST
EAT

PREVIOUS PAGE
Alexander Calder's Flamingo *at Dearborn and Adams near the Federal Building is not easily missed. Calder himself named it* Flamingo *because "it was sort of pink, and has a long neck."*

Civic Art: Jean Dubuffet called his Illinois Center work Monument with Standing Beast *(above). Some Chicagoans have considered Picasso's untitled sculpture (right) a woman, a dog, and a few other things. It is in Daley Center Plaza. Claes Oldenburg's aptly named* Batcolumn *(far right) is at the Harold Washington Social Security office at 600 West Madison. Jean Miro's* Chicago *(opposite) may be seen at the Brunswick Building plaza, across from the Picasso.*

The two lions standing outside the Art Institute of Chicago, sculpted by Edward L. Kemeys, have been on guard duty since 1895, two years after the building officially opened.

Two of the Art Institute's many treasures: The famous Sunday Afternoon on the Island of La Grande-Jatte *(top) by Georges Seurat, French neo-impressionist, and* The Assumption of the Virgin *by El Greco.*

LEAVES·TO·MANKIND·WHICH·ARE·DELIVERED·DOWN·FROM·GENERATION·TO·GENERATION·AS·PRESENTS·TO·THE·POSTERITY

The Cultural Center at 78 East Washington has books and reference materials in 124 languages (from Igbo to American Indian dialects). There are typewriters with keyboards in 10 languages, including Hungarian, Hindi, and Japanese.

Marina City's twin towers are apartments in-the-round, with a riverfront marina, restaurant, dry cleaner, grocery store, and health club.

Chicago's old and new architecture: McGaw Medical Center of Northwestern University (opposite). The federal jail (left). Neogothic against stark modern (below, left). Illinois Center (below, right), with its 160-foot rotunda, has been one of the sights of the city since it was dedicated in May, 1985.

The John Hancock Center (above and below), the tallest combined office-and-residential building anywhere in the world, is impressive when viewed either by moonlight or daylight. The building that houses the main branch of the First National Bank of Chicago (opposite page) soars above a sunbather.

The old Northwestern railway station has been replaced by a 40-story ultramodern station, shopping mall, and office building. Although it handles only commuter trains, 60,000 passengers rush through it daily.

5757 South Woodlawn Avenue. Almost immediately it attracted worldwide attention; it led to Wright's being commissioned to design the Imperial Hotel in Toyko in 1913.

The first Chicago School of Architecture was born of the Chicago Fire—and gradually died as a result of Chicago's 1893 World Columbian Exposition. Chief of construction of the fair was Chicago classical architect Daniel H. Burnham, the same Burnham who created Chicago's lakefront park system. With the help of imported eastern architects, Burnham designed the fair in the form of a "Great White City" of Roman classical buildings so dazzling that neoclassical architecture became the rage not only in Chicago but throughout America. Thus, we have the white terra-cotta Spanish renaissance skyscraper at the Michigan Avenue bridge known as the Wrigley Building (1921); the flying-buttressed Gothic revival Tribune Tower across the way (1925); and the replica of a Greek temple crowning the old Stone Container Building (1923) on the other side of the river.

Few buildings went up from the time of the Great Depression until 1950. But in the late 1930s and the 1940s, the second Chicago School of Architecture was born under the guiding genius of German refugee Ludwig Mies van der Rohe, dean of the School of Architecture of Chicago's Illinois Institute of Technology. As an architect and teacher and later as director of the Bauhaus, Germany's famed school of design, Mies van der Rohe had studied and kept alive the principles of the first Chicago School of Architecture. In 1938 he returned them to the city of their birth, enhanced, streamlined, married to modern materials. His strikingly spare, clean-lined designs, grids of glass and metal, can be seen today on the IIT campus on Chicago's South Side, in the Federal Center on Dearborn Street in the Loop, in the new twin Illinois Center buildings, completed after his death in 1969—in more than 40 Chicago structures. These, and dozens of other major Chicago buildings designed by his students and others influenced by him, make Chicago the architectural leader it is today. One example of his foresight is the sensuous 70-story glass-sheathed Lake Point Tower. Built by former colleagues in 1968, it resembles a 1921 Mies van der Rohe design that was never constructed.

The great Chicago architects of today are less public than the old masters, with the possible exception of Har-

Continued on page 128.

NBC Tower opened in mid-1989. The 37-story structure, six floors of which are leased to NBC, faces the river east of the Equitable Building.

There's something for everyone at the annual Gold Coast art fair. With such variety, every artist has a chance to sell something.

Warm-evening concerts in Grant Park draw throngs of music-and-mood lovers. The often star-sprinkled heavens, the proximity of Lake Michigan, and Kate Buckingham's colorful fountain add to the allure.

M
exit

OPPOSITE

Sun-dressed fans at Wrigley Field are known affectionately as Bleacher Bums. These stands are always filled, regardless of the Cubs' win-loss record.

Scenes from historic Comiskey Park, home of the Chicago White Sox. This stadium is being replaced by a new $100 million facility scheduled to open in 1991.

Winston
porter
JORDAN
23
SHARP
Reebok
AT&T

Michael Jordan, the air-borne Chicago Bull, has hang time so unbelievable that some night he may sail completely out of the Chicago Stadium. This high-flying superstar has rejuvenated Chicago's NBA franchise and has thrilled thousands of fans.

The Chicago Blackhawks are seen here practicing on their home ice at the Stadium. This NHL team consistently performs well in the Norris Division and for its hardy and loyal fans.

ry Weese, designer of the glistening copper-windowed Time-Life Building at Fairbanks Court and a leader in graceful restoration. Credit for modern landmarks is shared by teams of architects in such firms as Bertrand Goldberg Associates, which designed the 62-story "twin corncobs" of the Marina City apartments, and the giant Skidmore, Owings and Merrill, founded in Chicago in 1936 and now an international firm, with offices in nine cities. Skidmore, and others, are responsible for much of the thrill that comes from gazing at the Chicago skyline. Their credits include the John Hancock Center, the 110-story Sears Tower, the University of Illinois at Chicago campus, and the Richard J. Daley Center and Plaza (co-architects: C.F. Murphy Associates and Loebl, Schlossman, and Bennett). The 31-story Daley Center Building, Chicago's civic center, fittingly began in controversy. It was constructed of a type of steel designed to rust gradually into its present russet brown—an ugly process, many thought. The Daley Plaza, site of myriad activities—from protest marches to civic ceremonies—is dominated by Pablo Picasso's once-controversial sculpture in matching rusted steel. Chicagoans, unsure at first ("Is it a dog? Is it a woman?"), have now become very fond of it.

A complaint about Chicago's architects: There are too many good ones to record them all. This also can be said for Chicago's painters and sculptors. These include the Expressionist Rudolph Weisenborn; sculptor Lorado Taft (1860-1936), whose *Fountain of Time* graces the western end of the University of Chicago Midway; Franklin McMahon, a reportorial artist, and his son Mark, whose eight murals help brighten O'Hare; Aaron Bohrod, World War II *Life* magazine artist and master of trompe l'oeil (fool the eye) painting; and the Albright brothers, Ivan and Malvin. Several of Ivan Albright's exquisitely detailed but grimly realistic portraits may be seen at the Art Institute.

Chicago is home to a number of fine colleges and universities, ranging from city and community institutions to others that are world renowned. These include divinity, art, law, and medical schools, as well as Columbia College, which offers a liberal arts degree but specializes in turning out graduates headed for careers in radio and television.

The University of Chicago, Northwestern University, the University of Illinois at Chicago, Illinois Institute of Technology, and DePaul and Loyola universities perhaps are the best known. The University of Chicago, a rarity among major schools for having demoted football to the status of a sport, offers the usual curriculum plus a variety of special areas of study, and has been interna-

tionally famous, at least since the days of Robert Maynard Hutchins.

Northwestern is in nearby Evanston but qualifies for mention because of its downtown campus, which houses schools of medicine, dentistry, and law, as well as a division of continuing education where some 2,000 students attend night classes. The McGaw Medical Center of Northwestern University, with its several hospitals, makes this one of the largest concentrations of its kind in the city.

North Park College and Theological Seminary demands listing, as do Mundelein College, Chicago State University, Northeastern Illinois University, and the very popular city colleges. North Park has about 1,200 students and extension divisions on the South and Northwest sides.

Leads to some amazing and little-known aids to intellectual and physical stimuli may be found by scanning the Yellow Pages under the heading "Schools." Whether your desire is to give haircuts, become a concert pianist, cure cancer, earn a black belt in karate, or learn hypnosis, there is a school for you.

Chicago, in brief, is a city of infinite wealth and variety in its cultural and educational resources.

Soldier Field illuminated for a Bears night game, as seen from the roof of the McCormick Center Hotel. The Amoco Oil Building, John Hancock Center, and other skyline landmarks loom in the background.

The Chicago Bears shot from an interesting aspect during practice in Platteville, Wisconsin.

Aboard a helicopter is the only way to capture a photo like this of Wrigley Field, home of the Chicago Cubs and the last ballpark in the majors to install lights. Incidentally, this is also a great shot of downtown and Lake Michigan.

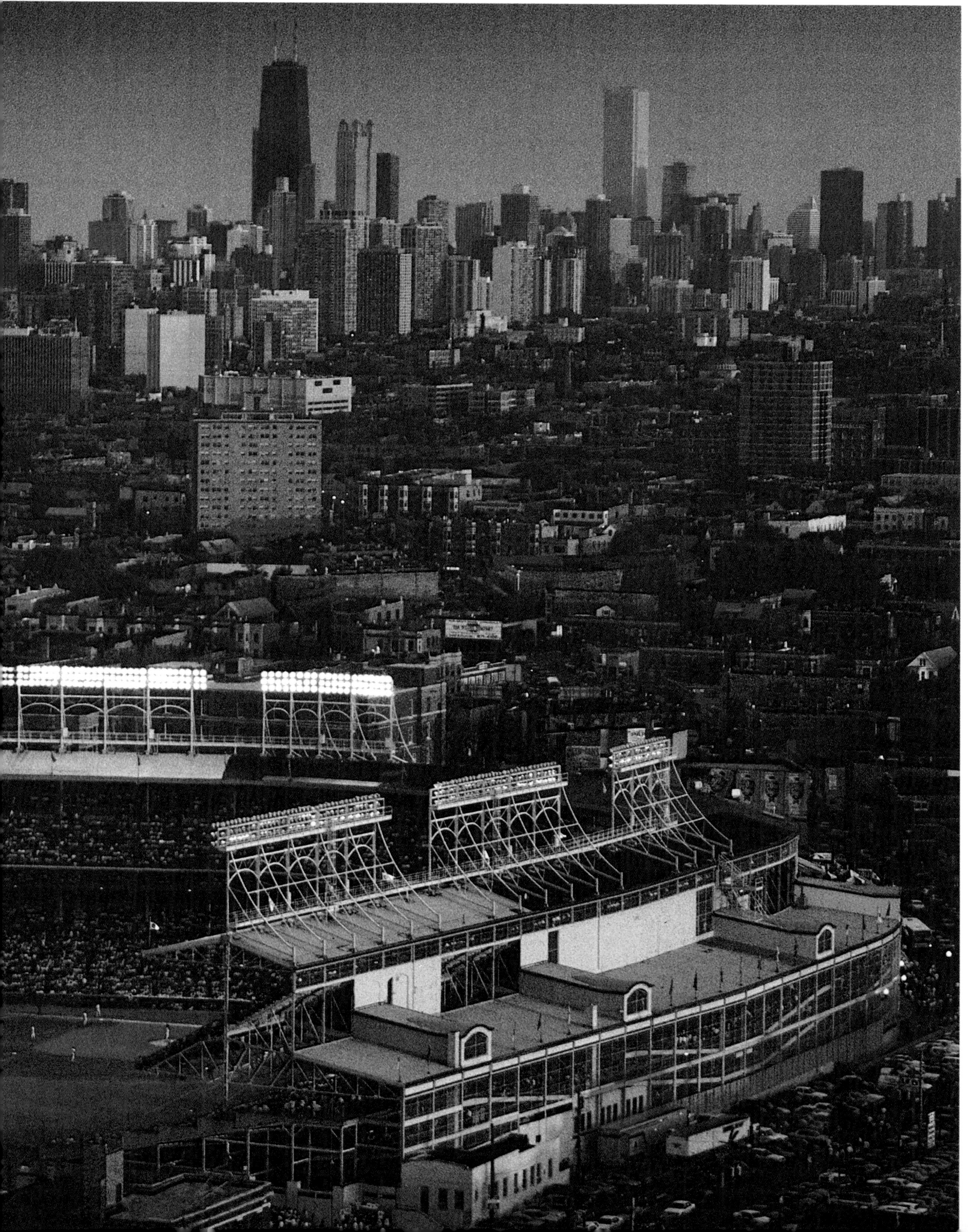

A local grandmother decided several years ago to give her grandchildren an autumn treat and erected this tableau in the yard on West Hubbard Street. It was such a success that she repeats the scene every year.

Chicago
PEOPLE & NEIGHBORHOODS

We have talked about various aspects of Chicago, without much exploration of what makes any city truly great: the people who live in it. Chicago consists of about 3 million persons dwelling within its boundaries and, on any working day, hundreds of thousands of others who come in to earn their salaries and who go home each night to Evanston, Mundelein, Wheaton, Flossmoor, and dozens of other suburbs that ring the city.

Many of these commuters moved from Chicago to the suburbs in recent years, helping to account for a drop in population of 600,000 since the 1950 peak. There are many reasons for the migration, including the desire for quieter and less-crowded surroundings and a wish, perhaps, to get closer to nature. But the proliferation of shopping centers, outlying theaters, and in some cases, the proximity of better schools, also added to the lure.

Yet even these suburbanites, whether they live a block from the city or 50 miles, basically consider themselves Chicagoans. They often shop in Chicago, take in a play, visit the museums and talked-about restaurants, attend White Sox games or watch the Cubs in beautiful Wrigley Field, and spend their Sunday afternoons each autumn screaming for the Bears. And when they are elsewhere—whether in Tacoma, or Tahiti, or Timbuktu—and are asked where they are from, they reply without hesitation, "Chicago!"

During THE winter of 1978-79, a number of Chicago-area residents developed cabin fever, or at least a bitter hatred of snow and ice. Many of these grabbed their furniture and the kids and headed south or west as soon as spring arrived.

But a reverse migration from the suburbs to Chicago has begun. A number of younger or older couples, often those without children, find something missing when they compare the easygoing life of the suburbs with the hum and bustle of the metropolis. They miss the lake and the neon and the taxi doors slamming, the restaurants, the theaters, the boutiques, and all the doormen at all those towering buildings. Others, as in Old Town and New Town on the city's North Side, find pleasure in reclaiming and restoring run-down mansions and entire neighborhoods to their old-time charm and vitality. All these have reversed the flow to some extent, and as the suburbs grow more like cities, with factories and late-afternoon traffic jams, the distinction between urban and suburban is becoming more and more blurred.

One reason Chicagoans like their city so much is the perennial feeling here that something good is about to happen. This seems to stem from the indisputable fact that Chicago is one of the world's great sports towns. The yearning of her long-frustrated fans for national championships for the White Sox, Cubs, or Bears—and it doesn't seem to matter much which one—hangs over the city almost like the smog that Chicago doesn't have much of anymore. It's a feeling most Chicagoans would miss. The craving was assuaged momentarily in 1985 when the Bears won the Super Bowl.

It also seems possible that Chicago remains alive and inviting because it hasn't yet melted down its thoroughly mixed population to turn each individual into a clone-like replica of all the rest, a tragedy that, it is devoutly to be wished, never will occur...

Typical adult Chicagoans are children or grandchildren of immigrants, or are immigrants themselves, not products of the Midwestern Corn Belt. Successive waves of the dispossessed and discontented have populated the city, beginning in the 1840s with the Irish fleeing the potato famine and the Germans whose hopes for freedom were dashed by the failure of the 1848 democratic revolution. Scandinavians followed in large numbers and lesser numbers of English, Welsh, and Scots. From 1880 to 1927, when immigration was sharply curtailed, most of the migrants came from eastern and southern Europe—Poles, Italians, Eastern European Jews, Bohemians, Lithuanians, Russians, Greeks, Serbs, Croatians, and Hungarians.

Even today it is said that Chicago is the largest Polish city in the world, except for Warsaw, the third largest Greek city, and fourth largest Croatian metropolis.

Jane Addams, whose Hull House at 800 South Halsted Street befriended and assisted immigrants of every nationality, described the conditions they faced in 1910:

The streets are inexpressibly dirty, the number of schools inadequate, the street lighting bad, the paving miserable....The older and richer inhabitants seem anxious to move away as rapidly as they can afford it. They make room for newly arrived immigrants who are densely ignorant of civic duties. Meanwhile, the wretched conditions persist until at least two generations of children have been born and reared in them.

Today, the prosperous descendants of these downtrodden folk live in their neat bungalows and two-flats and Gold Coast condominiums, and new immigrants have crowded into the old neighborhoods.

The end of World War II brought a great many displaced persons to Chicago. Most of these were from Europe, but others included Japanese aliens and Japanese-Americans from the West Coast who had been interned after Pearl Harbor, despite no indications of disloyalty, and who found it difficult or impossible to recover their former homes and businesses.

In more recent years, since the end of the war in Vietnam, Chicago has become a haven for fleeing Vietnamese, Laotian, Cambodian, and other refugee fam-

A Chicago police officer makes friends with a child in Albany Park, a Korean neighborhood on the city's Northwest Side.

ilies (in 1980 arriving at the rate of 500 persons a month). Add to these numbers the Russian Jews and Assyrian Christians escaping discrimination at home and the many technicians, managers, and professionals from various countries who have come to Chicago either as employees of foreign companies or simply to better their own lives.

Most migrants in the last 40 years have come from neither Europe nor Asia (although there are many refugees from Southeast Asia), but from the South—mostly blacks from Mississippi and nearby states, displaced by poor economic conditions and mechanization.

During World War II they were attracted to Chicago by defense plants seeking workers, and they kept coming in the years following the war. Today more than 1 million Chicagoans are blacks, living mostly on the South and West sides, but increasingly scattered throughout the city.

From south of the continental United States—from Mexico especially but also Puerto Rico, Jamaica, and Haiti—has come a strong new wave of migration. At least a quarter of a million Mexicans now live in Chicago, where many of them work long extra hours, as immigrants have always done, to help support family members in poor villages back home and prepare the way for *their* migration.

There are plenty of ethnic neighborhoods still left in the city, even though many are not sharply defined, where you can practice any of dozens of languages; eat food prepared as it is in half a hundred foreign lands; buy books, magazines, and newspapers you may not be able to read; or look through an ethnic museum that helps preserve the heritage no one wants to forget completely.

Storefronts and signs and a restaurant guidebook will provide clues to ethnic neighborhoods, as will the distinctive accents of spoken Spanish, Serbian, Bengali, or other languages. Perhaps you will find a Greek cafe just in time to see the belly dancer perform. Or you can assuage your hunger with Polish sausages, Italian cannelloni, or solid Bohemian fare. Take a drive up Lincoln Avenue or Halsted or Clark, counting the neighborhoods and languages and cuisines from Irish to Mexican, Korean, Peruvian, German, Argentinian, Swedish, Ukrainian, Thai, and then some.

You may wish to visit some of the churches, which were the focal points for the ethnic neighborhoods and, in some cases, still are. In most instances they are Roman Catholic. Most European immigrants came from Catholic countries, and Chicago is predominantly a Catholic city, as evidenced by the hundreds of thousands of the faithful who shared in the Mass celebrated by Pope John Paul II in Grant Park in the fall of 1979 and who watched the televised ceremonies at Holy Name Cathedral. There is ornate St. Nicholas at 2238 West Rice Street, which is the heart of a strong Ukrainian community. There is also the Midwest Buddhist Temple at 435 West Menomonee, which serves the Japanese-American population on the near North Side and helps sponsor a Japanese street fair that coincides with the neighborhood Old Town Art Fair.

There are other indications that Chicagoans are reluctant to sever their ties with the homeland, even though they may be a generation or so removed from it. One very obvious example is that the Chicago River is dyed green every St. Patrick's Day (this was started during the time of the first Mayor Daley and is being continued) and that there is a huge St. Patrick's Day parade, sponsored by the Chicago Journeyman Plumbers Union, Local 130.

The Puerto Rican community also has a beautiful and impressive parade each summer, with everyone welcome who wishes to come along. One of the city's oldest ethnic parades—and the third largest parade in the country—occurs annually on Bud Billiken Day, which was the creation more than half a century ago of Robert S. Abbott of the *Chicago Daily Defender,* one of the largest black newspapers in the nation. Bud Billiken is now a kind of good luck figure. The name was originally coined as a thank-you to the newsboys who helped Abbott in his early days. They became members of the Bud Billiken Club and were honored with a parade and picnic. The parade is eagerly awaited by the black population of Chicago and its environs. There are floats, bands, and eventually a picnic in Washington Park.

Chinatown, which is now the area bounded more or less by Cermak Road, 24th Street, Stewart and Archer avenues, and the Dan Ryan Expressway, had its beginnings late in the 19th century when Chinese who had worked on the transcontinental railroads began arriving in Chicago and settled near Clark Street and Van Buren. The encroachment of business firms forced a move around 1912, however, and the Chinese business people began to pick up property around 22d and Wentworth, where the new Chinatown developed.

The neighborhood of Chinese shops and restaurants, with its exotic signs and sounds, becomes even more alluring when it's time to celebrate the Chinese New Year or some other holiday. These festive occasions are observed by marching, fireworks, and ferocious-looking but friendly dragons.

The ethnic makeup of Chicago has strongly influenced its politics, as during the 20-year reign of Mayor Richard J. Daley, who was called "the last of the big-city bosses." When Mayor Daley was running things, Chicago was known as "The City That Works." But Daley died suddenly in 1976, and the legacy he left has become somewhat tarnished. There was no one to hold together the political machine he was so instrumental in building or the various factions of the city. Nor was there anyone left with his unique ability to soothe the unions.

Chicago's diversity and personality are reflected in each of these faces, including that of the late Bill Veeck, at right.

But on the other hand, nothing too bad has happened, despite a shortage of money and occasionally of tempers. Michael Bilandic succeeded Daley, and, hit by a bad snowfall which paralyzed the city during his term, Bilandic was succeeded by Jane Byrne. She in turn yielded to Harold Washington, the city's first black mayor, who died suddenly in 1987 during his second term. Alderman Eugene Sawyer served as interim mayor until a special election was held in 1988, which brought Richard M. Daley, son of the former mayor, into the office his father had held.

There are no guarantees about the future, of course, but Chicago has been around a good while. It has survived and prospered for about 150 years, which someone recently noted is only about 20 years less than the lifetime of Washington, D.C. So it is not, despite its brisk and unflagging pace, a new town. It is a town that knows its way around. If Chicago could be described in human terms, you would call it street-wise. It knows all the tricks—and the responses to them.

Chicago, in brief, is alive and well. And it looks as though it will be for a long time to come.

Judging by their faces and costumes, these young women (opposite) seem to like the annual Chinatown festival tremendously. Equal enjoyment, if more restrained, is shown by members of Chicago's Easter parade (above).

On St. Patrick's Day, everyone in Chicago is Irish. Well, nearly everyone. There are green hats, green carnations, and the river is dyed green. Rain, frequent in Chicago during March, never dampens this gala.

CHICAGO'S
ST. PATRICKS DAY PARADE
SONS of St. PATRICK

Lunch time has arrived at Chicago Place, an addition to the Magnificent Mile at Michigan Avenue and Superior Street.

Chicago's rich ethnicity is shown in part here: Puerto Ricans celebrate with a parade, and several Irish wrestle with a flag following another parade.

EW NAN
1974

A Mexican-American vaquero steals the limelight in an Ethnic Day procession, and Italian Americans are richly costumed for a Columbus Day observance.

Chinatown occupies a few square blocks on the South Side,
and the annual Chinatown fair draws huge crowds of every ethnic background.

A tremendous mass of runners turns out for the annual Chicago Marathon.

The Fiesta del Sol celebration is held at Blue Island and 21st Street early in August.

FIESTA
AUGUST
FEATURING MILLER GENUINE
Genuine Draft
Virgo
Centro Nacional de
ESPAÑOL de
AT&T
AT&T

Aunt Lucy's
SALAD MUSTARD

Rooftop basketball near the Northwestern station (center). Presidential Towers, one of Chicago's newest downtown residential highrises, looms on the left.

Chicago has many eating spots, including this stand across from the Lorado Taft statue on the University of Chicago Midway.

A quick photo-tour of city neighborhoods. Clockwise from top left: houses on the Near North Side; churches in ethnic areas; remodeled North Side apartments; former residence now a French language school; Calumet Park; and Chinatown.

218
Maison Francaise de Chicago

One of the curious features of Chicago is Cricket Hill. Where there used to be a cricket pitch, soccer fields now are found. The hill, in Lincoln Park, was created by the Chicago Park District in 1948. Today the hill is a place to walk, run, ski, sled, fly kites, lie in the sun, or—for youngsters—roll down.

Another day dawns on Chicago as the sun rises peacefully over Lake Michigan.

CHICAGO & VICINITY
CENTRAL CHICAGO
© 1990, 1980 Rand McNally
See map at right
LAKE MICHIGAN
Free Limited–Access Highways
Toll Limited–Access Highways
Other Four-Lane Divided Highways
Principal Highways
Other Through Highways
Other Roads
0 1 2 3 4 Miles
0 1 2 3 4 5 6 Kilometers
Chicago
North Chicago
Libertyville
Mundelein
Lake Bluff
Lake Forest
Highland Park
Deerfield
Northbrook
Glencoe
Winnetka
Wilmette
Evanston
Skokie
Glenview
Morton Grove
Niles
Park Ridge
Des Plaines
Mount Prospect
Arlington Heights
Palatine
Wheeling
Buffalo Grove
Prospect Heights
Rolling Meadows
Elk Grove Village
Bensenville
Wood Dale
Addison
Elmhurst
Villa Park
Lombard
Oak Park
Maywood
Cicero
Berwyn
La Grange
Brookfield
Downers Grove
Hinsdale
Westmont
Darien
Willowbrook
Burbank
Oak Lawn
Evergreen Park
Blue Island
Harvey
Dolton
Calumet City
Hammond
Whiting
East Chicago
Lansing
Munster
Highland
Griffith
Chicago Heights
Homewood
Flossmoor
Tinley Park
Orland Park
Oak Forest
Markham
Midlothian
Palos Heights
Lemont
Mokena
New Lenox
Lincolnwood
Chicago Ridge
Hickory Hills
Bridgeview
Summit
Alsip
Worth
Crestwood
Country Club Hills
Hazel Crest
South Holland
Glenwood
Lynwood
Riverdale
Robbins
Posen
Calumet Park